SCHOOLS
within SCHOOLS

SCHOOLS
within SCHOOLS
Human scale education in practice

Wendy Wallace
Photographs by Mike Goldwater

CALOUSTE
GULBENKIAN
FOUNDATION

Published by
Calouste Gulbenkian Foundation
UK Branch
50 Hoxton Square
N1 6PB
+44 (0)20 7012 1400
info@gulbenkian.org.uk
www.gulbenkian.org.uk

ISBN 978 1 903080 12 2

British Library Cataloguing-in-Publication Data
A catalogue record for this book is available from the
British Library

Designed by Pentagram and Helen Swansbourne
Printed by Expression Printers Ltd, IP23 8HH

Distributed by Central Books Ltd,
99 Wallis Road, London E9 5LN
T 0845 458 9911, F 0845 458 9912
orders@centralbooks.com
www.centralbooks.com

Cover: Brislington Enterprise College. Photo: © 2009
Wendy Wallace.

CONTENTS

FOREWORD

The Foundation's purpose, across all the areas in which we work in the UK, is to help enrich and connect the experiences of individuals, achieving maximum beneficial impact through lasting systemic change. Our record of over fifty years of progressive interventions of a social, educational or cultural nature bears witness to this ambition. And working through strong partnerships is an essential feature of effecting lasting change.

The 'Human Scale Schools' project, established in 2006 in partnership with the educational charity Human Scale Education, has sought to address fundamental failings in our current secondary education system – for all students, including those most in need of support. For the last two decades the debate in education has been principally about governance: who runs the school – whether they be academies, foundation schools, trusts. If we are to advance from the plateau of performance on which we in the UK are stuck, and avoid condemning a generation of young people to social and educational dislocation, we need now to move beyond this narrow dimension of the debate. We need to concern ourselves with something more fundamental and important: structure, design and organisation – how should schools be configured, what should they look, feel like, how should they work? And as with health and social care, personalisation is key.

The persistent increase in the number of large, impersonal secondary schools, particularly in the last decade, and growing evidence that students learn best in small-scale settings where they are known as individuals, were the incentives for the 'Human Scale Schools' initiative. Our aim was to help larger secondary schools address these problems by adopting different kinds of human scale practices. Our guiding principle was that the relationship between learner and teacher is of prime importance in enabling all young people, and particularly the disadvantaged, to fulfil their potential, and that such relationships thrive best in small-scale settings.

Our approach was to offer to schools grants of up to £15,000 to take time out from the hectic pace of the school day and reflect on ways in which they might become more human scale. This might include the creation of small learning communities or 'mini-schools', or developments in the areas of learning, student participation and community links. A special category of support offered help for schools that were part of the Government's Building Schools for the Future programme (BSF), since that provided a perfect opportunity to encourage such schools to incorporate human scale concepts into the design of their new buildings. It wasn't our intention that schools should in some way become smaller; rather, that they should re-structure into small-scale communities or adopt other practices that gave priority to the human scale in education.

Convinced of the relevance of human scale principles for *all* schools, we sent information about the project to every secondary school in the country. The response confirmed our conviction: we received over a thousand enquiries – nearly a third of secondary schools in England. The constraints on our budget meant that only 39 schools were ultimately funded, though this created a core of schools that could take the work forward and serve as examples to others.

Such statistics conceal a deeper truth. For schools, the adoption of a human scale ethos and the translation of this into practice is an enormously challenging enterprise. The vision needs to be conceived of and developed, the staff team needs gradually to be persuaded of its value and intimately involved in its implementation, students need to be involved and their views heeded, and parents need to be convinced of its value. That so many schools were ready to make this journey testifies to their commitment and courage and to their belief in the cause.

This book takes a close look at these different processes, focusing in particular on two schools funded by the Foundation as part of the Human Scale Schools project, one in advance of a move to a new building and the other both before and after it had made that transition. The author has an eye for the way in which momentous changes are accompanied by day-to-day matters. She depicts a head teacher contemplating the long-awaited move to a new building and conveys his concerns: 'There are insufficient lockers in the Year 9–11 communities. Despite swathes of colour distinguishing the com-munities – which they have decided to name after big cats – the new school is greyer inside than he wanted. The architects are known for their liking for grey. He rubs his eyes, thinking about numbers in the small canteen, how they will make it work.' It is this attention to the human detail of change that distinguishes the book, and is the manner in which the progress of the two schools – the advances, the set-backs, the moments of elation and despair, the courage of staff, the sheer dogged determination of the head teachers – is brought to life. The photo essay of students at Stantonbury Campus helps make the point: this is what change looks like on the ground.

The excellent response to the Human Scale Schools project, the high profile it has already achieved in the media and the growing number of BSF schools opting for human scale designs suggests that, in education, the large and impersonal is beginning to be rejected in favour of the small and human. The Human Scale Schools project has played its part in encouraging that process and so too, we hope, will this book. It will show schools who want to travel in this direction what the reality of change looks like. No less importantly, it offers companionship and encouragement to those who have chosen this path already.

Andrew Barnett
Director
Calouste Gulbenkian Foundation UK Branch

PROLOGUE

Human scale education usually refers to what goes on in small schools. In recent years, attempts have been made in large state comprehensives to adapt the principles and practices for the benefit of more students and teachers – as well as to redefine them for a changing world.

Supersized schools are nothing new; an early prototype existed at Hanwell in Middlesex in the nineteenth century and was dubbed the 'monster school'. Now, big schools are growing; England has 25 contemporary 'monster schools' – of more than 2,000 students, four times as many as a decade ago. There are 263 English secondaries of 1,500 to 2,000 students – twice as many as when Labour took office.

Large schools – with their cost effectiveness and potential for wide curricula – are likely to remain, but they do not have to mean an impersonal experience for children. The initiative to provide a small-school experience for children at big comprehensives began in the 1970s in this country at Stantonbury Campus in Milton Keynes, was notably brought forward at Bishops Park College on the Essex coast in the early years of the new millennium and now continues on a broader base.

Brislington Enterprise College in south Bristol is one of a number of schools taking advantage of the Government's Building Schools for the Future (BSF) programme to reconstruct themselves physically as schools within schools – and forge a practice to match. Some other schools are changing their structures and practice within existing school buildings.

why human scale?

Despite an ever-fiercer standards drive, education fails many children at many levels. Nationally, fewer than half achieve the five good GCSEs, including English and maths, that the Government has set as a benchmark; many leave with no qualifications.

Some young people enjoy school and do well there. But many do not. A stream of media items on childhood depression and suicide, on rising violence and alienation, tell as loud a story as the annual exam figures. While primary schools often succeed in containing and nurturing children with emotional problems, secondary schools tend to lose them fast. Truancy – despite draconian measures that include jailing parents – continues to rise. Many of the most troubled teenagers face permanent exclusion.

Few of these social ills spring directly from schools themselves. But schools are an opportunity to make some compensation for increasingly atomised families and communities, as well as to educate. 'School is the last, best sanctuary, the one place … where a student can trust that an adult is concerned for him or her,' wrote Professor Ted Sizer, a founder of the American small schools movement. In a context of rampantly commercial values, schools can offer alternative values, a place of belonging – and opportunities for all children to fulfil their potential.

Human scale education is not just for the disaffected. Successful small schools in the United States have offered great learning and development opportunities to gifted and talented students, as well as the self-excluding, and can provide a place of belonging for materially well-off but socially impoverished children. Former head teacher Mike Davies – whose Essex school embodied many of the values of human scale education – has written about the need to move away from a factory-like model of education, to redefine the purposes of education to fit the way we live and work now, for the benefit of all children. The national curriculum, he says, is 'remote and relentlessly redundant for large numbers of children.' Schools are still based on the way they were run for a very different world, a world of employment certainties that are now absent and a world without the readily accessible information that is now ubiquitous.

The basic human scale values – stress on positive student/ teacher relationships achieved within communities of not more than 250–300 individuals, on the central importance of children's wellbeing and voice in the institution, on enquiry-based learning that promotes skills rather than transmitting a body of knowledge – are finding resonance politically and culturally, with a proposed broadening of the primary curriculum, the abandonment of Key Stage 3 tests and recognition from the chief inspector of education that classroom boredom underlies some of the behavioural issues in schools.

how to create human scale?

For three years, the Calouste Gulbenkian Foundation, working with the charity Human Scale Education, has funded human scale projects in a number of English secondaries as well as research and development opportunities for school leaders.

Head teachers and staff from more than 20 secondary schools attended a conference in Nottingham in winter 2008 run by the Human Scale Schools project, a partnership between Human Scale Education and the Calouste Gulbenkian Foundation. Some of the schools are making adaptations to their practice and organisation; others are radically altering it.

These changes are given added potential impetus by the BSF programme, now in its fifth year. Under BSF, the intention is eventually to modernise every English secondary school.

This book – commissioned by the Calouste Gulbenkian Foundation – is an account of the aspirations and process in some of those schools. It looks at why some school leaders are seeking radical change in the culture, the factors that help and hinder such transformations and the progress made.

Brislington Enterprise College in Bristol has embarked on an ambitious project of whole-school transformation. Lister Community School in London's East End has initiated a pilot project with Year 7s to address the alienation and dip in performance that often accompany secondary transfer. Other schools – Stanley Park High School in Surrey, Walker Technology College in the North East and Glossopdale Community College in the Peak District have introduced a range of human scale measures to improve the experience and achievement of their students.

Students referred to or quoted in the text have had their names changed; in the photograph captions, names have been retained with the students' agreement.

CHAPTER ONE
The remaking of a school

Brislington Enterprise College – formerly Brislington School – lies on the edge of south Bristol, just off the A4 road to Bath, surrounded by streets of semi-detached houses on one side and on the other open countryside. Opened in 1956, Brislington's reputation has always centred on its size. Once the largest school in Bristol, with 1,650 students, sheer capacity was its defining characteristic. By the 1990s, parents saw it as too big – as a rowdy, oversized and impersonal institution. 'The only way my daughter would have gone there would have been over my dead body,' says one mother, of that time.

In 1999, the community's judgement was echoed by school inspectors. Ofsted decided that Brislington had serious weaknesses; the eight key issues to address covered everything from leadership to curriculum to teaching and learning.

Ironically, even as numbers fell, the school's negative reputation for being oversized remained.

The school pulled itself out of the failing category by spring of the year 2002; John Matthews – who had joined in 1999, as deputy head for ethos and values – became head at the beginning of 2003. He knew that no longer being a failing school did not equate to being a successful one. Persistently poor SATs results, disruptive behaviour and widespread truancy underlined the fact that some students were alienated, angry and underachieving. Was it the young peoples' fault? Or did it mean that the education on offer – the whole school experience, in fact – was not meeting the needs of a significant proportion of students?

This growing realisation that the school was letting down some students coincided with opportunity. In April 2003, leaders at the school realised they might join in the first wave of the national reconstruction programme, Building Schools for the Future (BSF). 'It straight away seemed to be about more than just a new building,' says John Matthews. 'The curriculum – and practices with young people – had to change.' In the shared office of the senior leadership team, they began to think about how.

The leadership at Brislington Enterprise College – John Matthews's two deputies Janine Foale and Ruth Taylor were appointed from within –

began to redefine what the school was about. The local authority wanted a new school for 1,775 students; this seemed to pose a familiar problem. 'If size was seen as an issue, what could you do about scale?' says the head. He and others went looking for ideas – researching, visiting other schools and attending conferences.

The small school movement in the United States inspired the team as a means of meeting both the social and learning needs of Brislington students, of making sure that some highly disadvantaged young people got a chance at school success. 'I come from a background that regards education as the route to an improved quality of life,' says John Matthews, whose family came from the Welsh valleys. 'But it has become harder for children from certain social backgrounds to move through.' Stronger relationships with adults and a more student-centred style of learning seemed to offer hope.

John Matthews and his colleagues committed themselves to rebuilding in the 'schools within a school' framework, aiming to create a small-school experience within a large institution. 'Very quickly,' says Mr Matthews, 'we were taking a coherent model to the bidders that said we would like communities of 300 children. We wanted to operate them as independent organisations within the whole.' By January 2005, construction group Skanska had been appointed to build a school where five separate 'houses' meet side by side along a generous, curving 'street' of shared space.

Alongside the communities was a planned range of shared spaces and facilities. Priority was given to the practical and creative activities – dance, sports, art and design, music and catering – at which many Brislington students excel. New technology was incorporated through-out and given its own areas.

A new building is not the same thing as a re-imagined school. John Matthews was determined that as a staff they would not be offering 'old wine in new bottles'. While workmen began to excavate foundations for the £34 million new school, staff began to construct a different learning approach. As a starting point, working with academics from the University of Bristol, as well as with staff and with students, John Matthews and his colleagues set out what they wanted the new school to be about.

Hope, trust, respect, enterprise and ambition emerged as the core values.

leaving school…

Fast forward to June 2008. It is the start of the last term in the old school building and the move, it appears, cannot come soon enough. In the leadership team office, tins of soup vie for shelf space with thank you cards and confiscated earrings. Worn out armchairs, an empty fruit bowl on the table, and piles of folders on the floor complete the picture. It is three months before the move and beyond a line of blue hoardings that carves the Brislington Enterprise College site in half, the long, low outline of the new school is taking shape.

Pinned to the back of the office door is what head teacher John Matthews calls the 'scores on the door'. These are Brislington's targets, in terms of Key Stage 3 tests, GCSE scores, GCSE A*–Cs including English and maths, GCSE passes at grades A–G, attendance – and fixed-term exclusions.

Brislington's attempt to make school a more meaningful and constructive experience for all children must be undertaken in the context of unprecedented Government pressure to squeeze up GCSE results. The extent to which these two imperatives pull in different directions will become increasingly clear over the next months.

Meanwhile, for this last term, deputies Janine Foale and Ruth Taylor are the acting leaders of the school. Head teacher John Matthews has been seconded to the building project, after the departure of assistant head Dave Schofield, who was previously managing the process.

It is a huge challenge to oversee the construction of a new school – and lead the creation of a new pedagogy and curriculum – at the same time as running a large and tumultuous existing school. Day to day issues facing the leadership team tend to crowd out strategic thinking time, in school hours at least. Pressing operational issues today are: decanting from the science labs in advance of the move to new premises, the absence of any timetables yet for next year, and – most immediately – a mother shouting down the phone, irate about her son's internal exclusion.

Ruth is busy placing ads in *The TES*; four teaching posts are unfilled. All three members of the leadership team are upset that a Brislington teacher has left to be head of maths at another Bristol school. An important part of making the transformation a success is getting and keeping the right staff.

But morale in the team is good. Numbers for next year are encouraging. Parents seem to like what they have heard about the plans for the new school. There are 179 new Year 7 students already confirmed, including a higher percentage than usual of families making Brislington their first choice. They'll end up with at least 200 new students, they believe – and they need to. The curriculum is modelled on an intake of 200–210 Year 7s.

a tour of the building...

By 15 September 2008, in three months time, the school community will move to the other side of the high blue fence. For now, health and safety requirements mean that access to the rising new building is strictly limited. But staff need to see the work in progress, in more detail than is allowed by small viewing windows cut into the hoardings. John Matthews conducts a tour of the building, for a dozen senior teachers dressed in hard hats, fluorescent vests, gloves, goggles and steel toe-capped boots. The outside is made of grey brick, which is cheap but not immediately appealing. 'Prison-like', goes up a mutter from the back of the tour.

Inside the skeleton school, the group seems awed by the audacious length and openness of the central street, its generosity of space. At 500 square metres, the embryonic library is the size of a small field; the sense of light and space could not be in starker contrast to the crumbling old school with its cramped corridors and disparate, dated, classroom blocks.

One community on the ground floor has been designed for 20 students with physical impairments; this and a 20-place unit on the first floor for children with autism make up to seven the number of mini-schools within the new school. The five mainstream communities, sited next to each other in a row off the main street, will consist of two for Years 7–8, two for Years 9–11 and one sixth form.

The first issue to prompt heated discussion is the lavatories; in the new building, students and adults will use the same facilities. This sends an egalitarian message but should they also be unisex throughout? A number of voices are raised in favour of separate male and female loos.

The party dons overshoes – a cross between shower caps and J Cloths – to go inside one of the planned communities that are the key characteristic of the new school culture. They stand in the 'social space' in the back of the house-like structure, stare up at the high atrium, at the empty labs and classrooms and a central stairway that feels almost domestic. The staff voice enthusiasm – and concerns, when it emerges in the course of the tour that there is no provision for adults to make themselves tea or coffee.

'It's because none of this is ours,' comments one. The building is being built under the private finance initiative (PFI), and will be leased from construction company Skanska for the days of the school year, from 8 am till 6 pm. But all of this must become 'theirs', at the level that matters, if the new school is to succeed.

changing culture...

Arguably the most complex challenge in reforming a school is to change adults' attitudes and practice. Some Brislington teachers believe in the move to human scale education, a minority are resistant and others lack conviction. 'Some teachers here are passive. They just want to come in and teach their subject,' comments one longstanding member of staff. Many, historically, believed that Brislington students could not be expected to achieve highly because of the social problems in the area.

Children have already learned a lot by the time they arrive at Brislington Enterprise College. A proportion have absorbed the message from society that they won't amount to much. Some arrive believing that the school failed their parents and other relatives and is likely to fail them. Many – usually working class boys – come without the reading and writing ability necessary to get to grips with the secondary curriculum; social and emotional problems are widespread.

Brislington students, like students everywhere, want to know that what they are learning will be relevant to them and their lives. 'It is very hard to motivate some students to do anything,' says science teacher Greg Seal. 'They don't see themselves going anywhere. A lot think they don't need school, to succeed.'

The experience of many of their heroes – whether from the music industry or sports world – appears to confirm the thinking.

John, Janine and Ruth, the leadership team, began in 2005 to try to alter what happens in Brislington's classrooms, influenced by the work of Professor Guy Claxton. Claxton coined the new '4 Rs' – resilience, resourcefulness, reflectiveness and reciprocity – as the qualities children need to develop as learners. 'Learning to learn' proved a useful starting point for curriculum reform and by the following year school leaders decided to go further and make skills the prime focus of the first year in secondary school.

From 2006, Brislington's Year 7 students have had sixteen hours per fortnight of themed, cross-curricular, humanities project work, based on the five competencies (CLIPS) of the Royal Society of Arts Opening

student voice

Ross, now 16 and in Year 11, describes the impact on him of altered teaching:

'In Years 7, 8 and 9, you've got to do languages and music. I didn't really like languages. I didn't get on with my teacher very well, so it was hard. I just used to sit at the back and draw and stuff. Half the time I'd listen, half the time I'd think about what I'd do later on, just to get away from it.

'If your teacher understands you, you're going to listen to them more and find it easier to talk to them. If they've shouted at you, you don't feel as confident around them, to ask questions. There aren't many teachers I don't get on with. I like teachers that you can have a joke with, as well as get on with the work.

'If you have to sit in silence, you don't want to concentrate. When you're enjoying yourself, you pay more attention. This year, I haven't been bored.

'Over the last couple of years, they've asked what kind of learner you are. When it's more entertaining, you'll listen. If it's interesting, what you're doing, you'll want to take part.

'I like the idea of more light in the new building. It'll feel nicer. More alive. I might come and do sixth form next year although I've applied to do plumbing and carpentry at another school. I'd like to do something more hands on. I did resistant materials, but our teacher had a heart attack. We just had supplies, for two years.

'I got a B, for the table I made. Ungraded, for my folder.'

Minds curriculum and taught by a limited number of teachers. The competencies emphasise the ability to understand and to do, rather than just the transmission of knowledge. They include citizenship, learning to learn, relating to people and managing information and situations. The aim was to equip Brislington students to become independent and confident learners – and reduce the alienation and boredom some felt.

The RSA Opening Minds curriculum has found resonance in many English schools; it has been taken up by more than 200 and the Royal Society has now sponsored its own academy. Skills-based learning requires teachers as well as students to approach learning differently. It needs joint planning between departments and a willingness on the part of staff to focus on skills rather than content. At Brislington, the shift towards skills – taught by a smaller number of teachers who actually know students as people – has begun to improve the experience of being in the classroom, students say.

staff questions...

In preparation for the move, John Matthews is hosting a series of informal meetings to answer staff questions. In a room with half a dozen adults – teachers and support staff – he reiterates the reasons for moving away from a content-driven curriculum to one that is skills-based. 'For a lot of our children, the experience of school is one of being told they can't do something,' he says. 'If I believed that what we were doing in the past was meeting the needs of our children – if I did – I wouldn't have changed a thing.'

Part of the plan for the new communities is for small learning families of about ten children to replace large tutor groups. The aim is for every child to have an adult who knows them really well and can act as a form of educational life coach. To make this possible, almost every adult in the school will become a learning guide. Most non-teachers, including Brislington's policeman, have agreed to take on the role. One clerical worker voices her unease about the prospect to head teacher John Matthews. She wants to take on the role, she says, but wants training to make sure she can do it well. Learning guides will get training, the head reassures her.

Maths teacher Mr Isaacs wants to talk about an old and intractable issue. Numeracy. 'Children are arriving at secondary school not knowing their times tables,' he complains. One of John Matthews's mantras is that since adults at the school cannot work any harder than they already do, they have to work differently. Part of the human scale vision is that children should be seen as learners in the round – rather than as a maths student in one lesson and an English student after break. In the new school, John Matthews tells the group, it will be the collective task of the communities to improve their children's numeracy and literacy, rather than the isolated responsibility of maths and English faculties. To make the point about the inter-connectedness of learning, John cites the case of a boy whose reading ability has barely improved since he came from primary school. 'He won't be successful in his GCSE science,' he says, 'not because he can't do science but because he can't read the exam paper.'

He closes the meeting on an immediate concern relating to the old building – making sure that departing it does not become an exercise in destruction. Huge levels of graffiti in the now-decanted science block have rung alarm bells. 'I have an absolute belief that we close this building with dignity.'

talk for prospective families...

Growing stronger and closer relationships with the community is a key aspect of human scale practice. But like many schools, Brislington has struggled in the past to work constructively with all its families. American educationist Deborah Meier neatly expresses parents' attitudes in an African-American district of Chicago. 'For many of the families ... the school was alternately ally and enemy. Parents couldn't assume that the people in the school viewed their child as an attractive, lovable and intelligent being.' This ambiguity is equally applicable to south Bristol. And, it might be added, teachers cannot assume that parents consistently see their children in that positive light either. 'Parents of some of our kids don't care what goes on as long as the kids aren't at home,' says a learning support assistant. 'A lot are single parents, with a lot of kids at home.'

It is a workable assumption that all parents fundamentally want the best for their child. And the fact that families like the idea of the communities – and their interest in the glamour and innovation of the expensive new buildings – is helpful ground on which to begin making closer links.

Parents turn up in ones, twos and threes on a June evening for a talk about the new school, held up two flights of stairs in the old library. It's mainly mums but two dads come and a few children. John Matthews shows them, on screen, the 190-metre-long, gently curving street that runs through the middle of the new school and that will house a small canteen at one end and two cafes at other points. Once children are in school, he tells parents, they won't be able to get out of the building until the end of the day; the main entrance is staffed and all the doors electronically controlled. The green dot on the plans represents the one protected tree on the site – an old oak.

He tells parents that the intent behind the changes is to raise the standards of attainment of every student, introduces the concept of Project – and deputy head Janine Foale takes over. 'If we just give a content-based curriculum, that's not sufficient for some of our students,' she begins...

The message about the reason for altering what goes on in the classroom must be transmitted again and again – to teachers, to support staff, to parents.

The team introduces to parents the idea of the learning families and John cites chief inspector of education Christine Gilbert's report on personalised learning, *2020 Vision*, which recommends the same practice. There is no doubt that in pursuing their own vision, Brislington leaders have anticipated the educational zeitgeist.

Parents, as ever, are mainly concerned about the immediate wellbeing of their own child. The first question from the floor is from a mother, concerned that girls will have to share lavatories with boys and men. John Matthews reassures her that the idea of having all the facilities mixed has been dropped.

Are the Year 7 and 8 communities split up by ability, asks a parent? No, comes the answer. Each community is mixed ability. Another mother complains that the children who don't want to work hold back the ones that do … and the team move the discussion swiftly on; they want to accentuate the positive. 'You will have to tell us in November, December, January – if it's working for you,' says John.

Thirty parents have arrived for the meeting, by the time it ends. Janine Foale is pleased with the modest attendance. It is better than the one or two people they have had in the past, she says. What frustrates them is parents who criticise the school – but won't come and see for themselves what happens inside the walls, or get involved in trying to change it.

Janine Foale thinks the school culture is already becoming more positive, even in advance of the move. She cites straws in the wind. Historically, the baubles were smashed off the Christmas tree as soon as it was put up in the school foyer. Last year, that didn't happen. McDonalds were always calling, from the drive-in across the A4, to complain about kids. They don't hear from them now. Teachers were afraid to do bus duty. Attendance is improving...

visits to feeder primaries...

At St Anne's Park Primary, a sunny, plant-dotted oasis in a deprived part of Bristol, transition manager and geography teacher Heather Evans paints an idyllic picture of life at Brislington Enterprise College: of mosaic club, batik club, and every sport known to boy or girl. Except rowing, she says. 'Because we're not near water.' She tells the group of Year 6 children sitting on the carpet in front of her what they might do if they are worried about bullying – how they can text or put a note in a special box, if they want to tell a teacher something but don't want to say it in person.

Heather Evans – enthusiastic, young and genuine in her care for the children – has accepted an acting leadership role in the new school, sharing the post of head of Panther, one of the two communities for Years 7 and 8. She tells the children that the big school is a bit like a nearby shopping mall, Cribb's Causeway, with its indoor/outdoor space. 'It's kind of a mini-school within a school. You've got a card to get into your own little community.' Year 6 listen, entranced. But their concerns seem very adult.

'How much is the uniform?' they want to know. 'Where do you get the bus?' 'I'm living with my auntie at the moment, and she's working,' says one. 'Does that mean I won't get free school meals?

In the primary head teacher's office, Heather is briefed about individual children. The Year 6 teacher is worried about Sonny. 'He's a nice kid, very funny, addicted to football. He can be incredibly rude, so rude that it won't be tolerated by you guys. If it's something he doesn't want to do, or doesn't agree with – that's when you'll see it.'

The area – St Anne's Park – is notorious for its poverty. The knock-on effects on children – and their relationship with school – are profound. 'There's a lack of self-esteem,' says the head, 'and a feeling that being from St Anne's, you can't survive anywhere else.' Amongst her children's parents, she says, there are 'phenomenal health problems, of all kinds'. 'Of 28 recent home visits, to new children starting in nursery, almost none had what we would consider a safe room for a child, with a fitted carpet, the door on its frame ... I'm not surprised so many parents are on antidepressants.'

The head will send a teacher from the school with the new Brislington students on their first day, to boost their confidence. 'We send you some lovely kids,' she tells Heather Evans. 'But the most noticeable thing about this area is that you have to assume that everyone has a heightened level of anxiety about everything.'

community links...

Brislington Enterprise College is already a school skilled in dealing with student anxiety and anger. Staff support worker Jane Graydon – with her roots in the community, her knowing kindness – is an important figure around the school. Never without her walkie-talkie, she is called out to help teachers contain behaviour that they cannot manage alone. Disruptive behaviour is a serious problem, with a minority of students causing a disproportionate amount of teacher stress and interrupting the learning of others.

Jane answers a call to an isolated Portacabin where a supply teacher has lost control of a Year 9 class, with one child up on the roof. The boy has come down by the time she arrives but several others are in an overexcited state, squeezing behind the metal handrail alongside the Portacabin, banging on the window, getting each other in headlocks. She wades in without hesitation. 'You! Get back in the classroom! Daniel! Sit down!' The supply teacher has entered into an ill-advised battle of wills with a girl over a plastic bottle of soft drink, trying to make her put it in the rubbish bin. Jane swipes it, saying the girl can have it back later.

Jane Graydon's four children attended Brislington school, and before that so did she – and her husband. She first got involved with the school when her youngest son was under threat of permanent exclusion. 'I offered to come in and sit with him. I knew moving him to another school wasn't the best thing for him. There's more now in place, than there was for him. If parents realised they could challenge the school, more would.'

The boy who at the Portacabin door was surly and stiff-faced is calm by the time she's walked him over to the canteen for an early break, joshing him out of his proud anger, her arm round his shoulders. By the time she leaves him, he's smiling, his anger dissipated. How does she do what many teachers can't? 'I've got a relationship with the kids,' she says, 'so it's easier for me to pick them up. I know about their lives. They don't have to explain everything to me.'

Jane Graydon began looking after her own younger brothers and sisters at age 12, when her mother – an alcoholic – left. The school knew nothing about what was happening for her at home. The walkie-talkie crackles into life. She's called to escort a girl off the premises. 'Wait till you hear the gob on her,' she says. 'Loads of issues. Mum's a drug addict.'

They will lose something when they decant. The old building may be leaking, peeling, crumbling, rotting. But there is a wild tangle of roses, marigolds and poppies around the onsite ICT facility belonging to the local authority; the inclusion base is a safe, tucked-away place to lick wounds sustained in the classroom; the very fabric of the school is scarred by the kids, their parents, cousins, aunties and uncles. It belongs to them. The newbuild, resolutely, belongs to Skanska. And in it, everyone says, there is nowhere to hide.

restorative justice…

Part of the changing culture at Brislington is a desire to move towards less confrontational forms of discipline. In the inclusion unit room, called I-base – Jane Graydon and one of her colleagues conduct a restorative justice session to try to resolve problems between a learning support assistant and a group of Year 9 boys.

'Do you know what restorative justice is?' she asks. 'You're all here today to put to an end the issues you have with "Mrs Jones", and the issues she has with you.'

Craig complains that the learning support assistant is unreliable. 'She lies. She says I've said swear words and that.' 'She don't stop moaning,' says another. 'When Matthew said he was dying, she said "do it quietly".' They call her Grass, because she takes notes. It is difficult for the woman, in front of two adult colleagues, to field the boys' criticisms. There are seven boys here, now. 'You're annoying. You're very annoying,' one says to her. But the opportunity for the students to express their views in a contained framework – and perhaps to consider the view of the other – is a learning experience in itself.

Mrs Jones insists: 'I'm not picking on you. I'm trying to help you.' The lads burp, tip their chairs, scratch themselves. Aidan is falling out of his shirt, out of his trousers, out of his shoes. They begin to talk about mobile phones.

Jane Graydon brings it back to the point. 'You don't have to like everybody, all the time,' she says. 'Sometimes you just have to tolerate them.' If they dislike Mrs Jones's style of working, what can be done?

'Don't get in our face first thing in the morning,' one says. 'While I'm working, leave me alone,' says another.

'What lessons are the hardest?' asks Jane.

'Every single one,' murmurs one of the boys, chucking bits of chewing gum to his friends.

'They resent me for being there,' says Mrs Jones. 'They just want to be able not to work.' A second meeting is scheduled, for the end of the week. If the boys refrain from calling her Grass, Mrs Jones will make them a cup of tea next time they come. Jane Graydon will buy the biscuits.

These are the most recalcitrant group of Year 9 boys in the school, Jane says, when the session concludes. She analyses who, of the seven that were in the room, has the respect of the other kids. Wraith-like Danny does – because of his older brothers. Not plump, unhappy Craig, whose mother has just taken up with yet another abusive man. Not soft Aidan, with his peroxided hair. Martin does, because of his height.

Most of these boys live with single mums, says the head, later. 'They are horrible to their mothers, and to their grandmothers. They have no men in their lives who are not abusive to women. Their mothers come to the school and weep in the office.'

special needs and human scale...

The proportion of students at Brislington Enterprise College with special needs is high and rising. Lynette Newman, director of student services, is on her mobile trying to get through to someone at the local authority, looking for help for a boy with autistic tendencies – but no statement of special needs, or the help that that brings.

The boy has twice reacted violently to other students in the classroom. After the second incident – in which he threw a chair, and another child was hurt – other parents want him out of the school. The school has been paying £300 per week for a learning support assistant for him, while they work out a strategy. But with new academies all around, bent on establishing reputations for discipline, no other school is likely to want to give him a fresh start.

'He needs the protection of a statement, or he could easily be criminalised,' says Lynette Newman. 'He's 12 years old and he doesn't know what's happening to him.'

Leadership at the school is 'unwavering' in its support for inclusion, she says. 'But thresholds for staff are lower than mine.' She is also child protection officer at the school. 'There are some things that as much as you want people to understand, you can't say.'

Lynette Newman is hoping the load will be better spread in the new building, where each community has its own pastoral team. But there are no cheap or short-term fixes for children's problems. 'Every time there is something not right for them – parenting, bereavement, abuse – you're presented at school with behaviours. As we get better at finding out what the issues are, the resources we need are bigger. And where do they come from?'

She believes there will be more chance of making a difference to children in the new school. 'Relations between adults will be closer. And between adults and children. We may be able to identify and deal with things sooner. We're very reactive, currently.'

The kids at Brislington are great, she says. 'They are straightforward. They want to do well. There are an awful lot of endearing things about them. But they don't trust. They're unsure of their identity...'

student voice

Louis, 16, is lanky, shaven, pale-haired. He is leaving Brislington Enterprise College on Friday, 'never to come back', he says. But although Louis will probably leave without the exam passes that would officially qualify his school life as a success, Brislington has been important in his life, providing stability at points where it was lacking elsewhere.

'In Year 7, I was small and shy. I didn't want to talk to get noticed. There were a lot of bullies. My first week was hell. But Year 7 was my best year here, as soon as I got to know my way round.

'Years 7 and 8, I can honestly say I was a good kid. Years 9 and 10, I turned around. My mum died. I started taking loads of drugs. Cannabis, cocaine, lots of stuff. I didn't really buy it, I just seemed to acquire it. I still smoke weed to this day.

'I've had three serious fights in school, two of them with the same kid. I'm alright with him now. The other fight was with someone who wasn't a member of the school, and it was broken up by a load of PE teachers. There are groups of kids who walk round aimlessly, don't go to lessons. They might as well stay at home in bed. There's groups within every year that are exactly the same. Bunking, looking for fights. Strung out on drugs.

the new teaching...

Some teachers have embraced the move to skills-based learning with enthusiasm. Ryan Lewin is one of them.

'Welcome to Mr Lewin's learning lab', reads the sign on the door of his geography classroom. The objective of the lesson is to use noticing and reasoning skills to explain the link between GNP and development, he has written on the whiteboard.

There are 31 students in this Year 9 top set. There are a lot of clever kids here, he says, but many don't like writing. 'They're verbal responders.' One loud boy, he says, would be in the bottom set in another school because of his behaviour. 'He's not writing now. But he'll give me a vocal answer.' And – as a rapid-fire question and answer session ranges over fair trade, over primary, secondary and tertiary industry – he does.

'My role has changed,' says Ryan Lewin. 'I put stuff in there, and show them how to do it. It's the how, not the what.' Is it a better way?

'Some of the teachers in this school are brilliant people. They'll listen to you, talk to you as an adult. And they'll handle a situation really well.

'Some teachers are just useless. My English class was full of norzers; the teacher walked out in tears. That's something you don't really expect to see in a grown man. He had a breakdown or something.

'At the end of Year 10, I realised I didn't have long to get it together. My dad and some of the teachers motivated me. I asked the teachers to give me the work. I redid pieces of coursework. When I took in what I'd done, they'd read it, and talk to me about it.

'When I was kicked out of home, John Matthews and the head of year gave me their mobile numbers. Did little things to help me. I don't want to disrespect the people who've helped me in my hour of need. I don't terrorise the school. When I see kids swearing at teachers, I say to them – "where do you think that's going to get you?"

'I am taking GNVQ science and GCSEs. I reckon I'll pass English and maths, because I redid all my coursework and got 2 Cs, B and A. I can guarantee I'll fail science, because I haven't been for about a year. Sometimes, it's not a fact of "I hate that lesson." Sometimes it's more a fact of "I hate that teacher."'

'No question. In humanities, it seems to work. We like to see ourselves as a little bit of a beacon. Because what are you in teaching for? For them? Or for yourself?'

'Next year is going to be awesome,' he says. 'Everyone's so up for it, everyone's going to want to push hard to make it work. Lots of people are really energised.'

Age 33, Ryan Lewin is doing an MA at the University of the West of England, on raising achievement in inner city schools. He used to work in a small school in Bristol, until the local authority closed it. 'Here we are, trying to recreate it,' he says. 'Small is better. Teaching is 75–80 per cent about relationships. If you know people, you can influence them. When do kids get into trouble? When it's people they don't know, supply teachers.'

In 2007, only 15 per cent of white working class boys in England got five good GCSEs including maths and English, compared to just under half of all students. A study from the University of Warwick's Institute of Education found the most significant influences on white working class achievement were children's aspirations for their own future, their self-confidence and their parents' aspirations for them. The white working class boys had less self-confidence than any other ethnic or gender group. These issues all spring into life at Brislington, inside and outside the classroom.

Some kids seem to have 'no buy-in' to the academic side of things, says Ryan Lewin. 'Parents are the same, often. I don't know whether that's because they've failed at it, in the past. We're a practical, suburban area, historically, of trades. They didn't stay on at school, and they don't see why the kids should.' The emphasis on finding things out, on managing information, engages students more effectively. 'When in doubt,' he says. 'Use the word "how". The new techniques are not revolutionary but they involve a lot of collaboration; that's what we've been weak at, historically.'

outstanding issues...

As the long-awaited move draws close, John Matthews still has nagging issues regarding the building. There are insufficient lockers in the Year 9–11 communities. Despite swathes of colour distinguishing the communities – which they have decided to name after big cats – the new school is greyer inside than he wanted. The architects are known for their liking for grey. He rubs his eyes, thinking about numbers in the small canteen, how they will make it work.

And he has larger concerns. 'Have we been able to move the teaching and learning model, enough? Have we got people far enough?' the head asks, rhetorically. They are three years in to the process of curriculum change and his assessment of their progress on a scale of 0–10 is that they're not higher than 6. There is still a broad swathe of 'satisfactory' teaching going on in Brislington's classrooms, predicated on content, and relying on traditional teaching methods.

Changing teaching is a slow and uneven process in any school. It requires courage on the part of teachers – to move away from the dollops of content that they used to dish out, and that most younger teachers were fed themselves, at school, since the introduction of the National Curriculum in 1988. It means departments co-operating with each other in new ways, individuals working together and sometimes teaching outside their own subject area. It demands time and resources. Most of all, it requires commitment from teachers, a belief among staff that it is the right thing to do. Teachers from other schools

student voice

As they reach the end of their time at the school, two high-achieving Year 11 students have mixed feelings about the proposed change at Brislington Enterprise College. Despite the new building's improved post-16 facilities, all are headed elsewhere for sixth form college. A key aspect of the reculturing of the school is to promote closer relationships between students and teachers. As the students speak, the importance they attach to relationships with their teachers becomes clear.

Indira, 16, is going on to study for A-levels in economics, physics, maths and geography. But she describes the many changes she has experienced in the old building in terms primarily of staff turnover. She and others in her year group suffered from having three ethics teachers in one year, she says.

'They come for a while and they end up leaving. Some of the students are too much for them. One teacher only stayed two months. Then another did a bit of work with us. By that time, everyone was just slacking. The teachers that stay form a bond. They're strict, but they've formed a bond.'

Indira is close to new ethics teacher Ann-Marie Abbotts, and geographer Heather Evans. 'Everyone would have failed if it wasn't for Miss Abbotts. And Miss Evans is always there to help us. She's really supportive. You can talk to her about friends, family, personal life.'

'Young teachers are nice. They don't go on about their children. They know what you're going through, because they've just been through it. Older ones, they refer to their own life. It's not what we need to hear.'

Janine, 15, says not all students want to be close to teachers. 'A lot of students in the younger years aren't willing to have that. They can't talk to them about anything else than work, because that's supposed to be their teacher, not their friend. They think it's gay or something.' Janine will study maths, economics, law and sociology.

that have introduced skills-based learning agree in Internet discussion forums that this last point is non-negotiable.

At Brislington, the message from John Matthews is steady. 'We can't change the culture by excluding a percentage of children. We have to generate the mechanisms by which these young people can be successful.'

Brislington's context is one of pressure, from within and without. As a local authority, Bristol is under pressure from the Department for Children, Schools and Families (DCSF); its GCSE pass rate and standards at Key Stages 2 and 3 all compare unfavourably with regional and national averages.

Brislington Enterprise College in turn is under pressure both from the Government and the LA to push up the exam pass rate. John Matthews does not disagree with the GCSE aims. 'I have to be robust with the standards agenda if that is the only model by which the school is judged. I am 100 per cent comfortable for us as a college to be held accountable.'

John holds fast to the vision of a student-centred school, where young people are empowered to take charge of their learning and follow their interests. But the standards agenda squeezes the school back towards the tried and tested methods that – viewed from a broader perspective – have failed so many here and elsewhere. 'It has forced teachers to adopt bite-sized content,' he says. 'The children are like fledglings in the nest; we force feed them what they have to know.'

leavers' breakfast...

It's the last day of school for Year 11. Students turn up in high spirits for their leavers' breakfast, their white school polo shirts scrawled with signatures, with slogans and hearts and kisses, their hair in multi-coloured ribbons, like May queens. They have whistles, face paints, and one or two have vodka in their Coke bottles.

Indira's there, cheerful in her jeans. One girl is dressed as a policewoman although in her micro shorts and fishnets, her rakish cap, there's not much danger of her being taken for a colleague of the school's police constable. Some are dressed like Skanska builders, in yellow hard hats. Two Somali girls are in special sequinned headscarves, the sleeves and hems of their black *abeyas* embroidered with gold thread. They lean their faces together, for the flash of a throwaway camera. One girl's T-shirt slogan could stand for all of them. 'Relax. Your [sic] amazing. You'll do great.'

PC Keith Hobden is out patrolling nearby front gardens, for alcohol concealed by students among the newly flowering rose bushes, the straggly privet. The free leavers' breakfast is a fatty offering of burgers, bacon, sausages and baps, which should line their stomachs against the later onslaught. In the canteen, a hubbub of excited voices is pierced by the random shrill of whistles – the PE teachers look discomforted. There's a Year 11 leavers' film, made by students, playing on the wide screen.

As John Matthews stands in front of them, the chatter ceases. 'You're the best performing year group that's ever been through this college. You all need to recognise how special that makes you as individuals, how special it makes you as a group. It's important that today, every single one of you stays safe. Thank you for everything.' The first tears are shed – by Heather Evans, trying to maintain her eyeliner.

The film is of individuals waving goodbye. It's touching and funny and already looks like history. As it ends, the Year 11s leave the premises. 'I've always been a bitch to you. I'm sorry,' one girl says to a teacher, as she walks out into the sunshine.

On 21 August, this last batch of students to emerge from the old Brislington Enterprise College will get their results. Three weeks later, the school will move into its new home and try to offer a new generation of students a radically different experience of education.

CHAPTER TWO
What is human scale education?

Founded in 1985 by a group of English educationists, the guiding principles of the human scale education movement are that school becomes most meaningful where relationships between teachers and students are strong and positive – and that this is best brought about in small communities, where students learn with a limited number of teachers who know them well. 'Small schools and small-scale learning communities enable the individual to strive for dignity and self-worth,' writes Mary Tasker, one of the founders of the UK movement and chair of the Human Scale Education charity. 'They also enable him or her to grow in a framework of caring for each other, their community and the environment.'

The human scale education movement took its inspiration from German economist E.F. Schumacher's classic text 'Small is Beautiful' and from a small schools movement in the United States that aimed to get away from impersonal, factory-like high schools that processed students through the system but were not responsive to their individuality.

The Coalition of Essential Schools (CES) was a network of schools inspired largely by the principles set out by American education reformer Ted Sizer. Ted Sizer was a teacher, then a teacher trainer and later chair of education at the Ivy League Brown University, in Rhode Island, until the late 1990s. He was briefly principal, with his wife Nancy, of a small school. His books – *Horace's Compromise*, and *Horace's Hope* – look at American high schools from the perspective of 'Horace Smith', Sizer's every-teacher. Horace has an enduring passion for teaching and for young people, but teaching hundreds of students – to a test-driven, standardised educational model – means he is not able to fulfil his vocation effectively. 'The traditional assembly line metaphor for schooling does not work,' Horace decides.

While *Horace's Compromise* looks at the high school status quo, *Horace's Hope* is Sizer's investigation of many inspiring and practical examples in the United States of how things can be different.

Professor Sizer's non-negotiable starting point was that 'one cannot teach a student well if one does not know that student well … the heart of schooling is found in relationships between student, teacher and ideas.' Ted Sizer proposed that teachers perceive themselves as generalists first and specialists second, that they work with no more than 80 students.

The Coalition of Essential Schools is informed by a set of principles that outline a coherent framework of values and practice and begin with a simple idea – that schools should focus on helping young people to learn to use their minds well. They include the idea that 'less is more', that depth of knowledge is preferable to breadth and that schools should be institutions based around the paradigm of the student as a worker rather than the idea of the teacher as a deliverer of instructional materials.

Deborah Meier is another leading American practitioner in human scale education, and a colleague of Sizer's. Her description of contemporary education in the United States – in an era of unprecedented reliance on testing – could equally be applied to the English experience. 'Learning about the world has been translated, even for 4-year-olds, into formats conducive to evaluation by standardised tests,' she writes, in her radical classic *In Schools We Trust*.
     Deborah Meier potently expresses a larger vision of what it might mean to teach children. 'For children, there is no shortcut to becoming thoughtful, responsible and intellectually accomplished adults. What it takes is keeping company with adults who exercise these qualities in the presence of adults-to-be.'

present identity...

American schools are different from English ones and on both sides of the Atlantic, information technology continues profoundly to alter the educational landscape, in a way that even young adults find hard to keep pace with. But the principles forged in the Coalition of Essential Schools endure. In adapted form, they have transferred to the UK movement. Mary Tasker defines the eight key ideas of human scale education in the United Kingdom as:

Small size – involving schools or learning communities of 250–300 students
Small teams of between four to six teachers, learning mentors and learning support assistants, who will see only 80–90 learners each week
A curriculum that is thematic, cross-disciplinary and holistic
Flexible timetable, with blocks of time, making provision for whole-class teaching, small-group teaching and individual learning, with teacher planning and evaluation timetabled

Pedagogy that is enquiry-based, experiential and supported by ICT

Assessment that involves dialogue, negotiation and peer review and develops forms of authentic assessment such as portfolio, exhibition and performance

Student voice – involving students in the learning arrangements and organisation of the school

Genuine partnership with parents and the community

Underlying the principles of the movement is a question that goes mainly unasked. What is education for? In the USA, Professor Sizer remarks that while agreement on the role of school is more straight-forward at primary level – all children need a chance to acquire at least the basics of literacy and numeracy – it is less simple to agree a vision of the purpose of secondary schools. 'It is easier to get on with the familiar … far harder and certainly more painful to step back and ask what all this is for in the first place.'

Currently in England, the Government agenda signals that secondary school is for the acquisition of five GCSEs or equivalent at grades A*–C, including English and maths, to sooner or later fit the student for the workplace. But feedback from employers is that school is not fitting many young people for employment – that real-life jobs require young people able to co-operate, take the initiative and trust in their own creativity. 'The lifeblood of British schools has become choked by a regime that frogmarches children through exam after exam, leaving them bereft of the skills they need to get on in the world beyond the school gates,' writes independent sector head teacher and thinker Anthony Seldon. Even universities complain that many undergraduates are not equipped for independent study and self-direction.

Mary Tasker suggests a perspective that is wider, deeper and more meaningful. 'For Human Scale Education the purpose of education is the development and growth of the whole person – creatively, emotionally, socially, morally, and spiritually as well as intellectually – and the achievement of a fairer and just society.'

Mike Davies, another founder of the UK movement, was at Stantonbury Campus in the 1970s and went on to lead a radical phase in the life of Telegraph Hill comprehensive in the south London borough of Lewisham before heading a new purpose-built school on the Essex coast. Bishops Park College under Mike Davies was unique as a truly radical state school. Built as three 'schools within a school', Mike Davies's vision was of an egalitarian community where students found and grew their talents and their selves.

To create this was demanding. The area was deeply deprived socially, the third poorest in England. Most families had a history of school failure over generations. But that history created opportunity. Parents wanted change, says Mike Davies, and so did the local education authority. 'There was a tacit understanding that it was OK to be different.'

Bishops Park was unmissably different. Teachers worked in small, cross-curricular teams with fewer than 80 children; relationships were put at the heart of the institution. There was no streaming or setting. Subjects were woven together, taught through themes. Block timetabling, in the form of three consecutive faculty days each half term, gave scope for in-depth learning.

But what really distinguished Bishops Park was something more intangible – a sense of freedom and possibility, rarely found in schools, that communicated itself to visitors both through the friendly, open students, the democratic atmosphere of the school communities, the range of things going on. Clubs at lunchtime and after school – 26 of them in total, in chocolate-making, juggling, trampoline, 'room in a box' model-making – were a non-negotiable part of the day but allowed children choice. Fridays were given over to all-day master classes – in subjects ranging from cake-making to probability to narrative poetry, run by teachers to reflect their passion for their subjects. 'Good attendance is mainly due to the interesting and relevant curriculum', commented Ofsted inspectors, one year after the school opened. Bishops Park is perhaps the only English school that a child has ever broken into out of hours not to vandalise or torch but for somewhere to sleep, until the storm at home passed.

It was no part of Mike Davies's vision that essential skills or qualifications be neglected. But he was interested not in what he calls the 'GCSE sprint' but in laying foundations for lifelong learning. 'My view was that we had to nurture those kids for a marathon. I wanted them to feel good as people, and to get better and better as learners.'

Mike Davies's passion for human flourishing, his vision of a school that offered 'dignity, challenge and excellence' sat uneasily with the bureaucratic and test-driven Government model. While a first Ofsted inspection was positive the second one, shortly after he left, was highly critical. Bishops Park was put in special measures by Ofsted in 2007 and under the leadership of an executive head teacher looks set to become an academy. The spirit of the school according to those who still teach there, has changed utterly.

Human Scale Schools project…

It is difficult for school leaders in the current climate in England to ask – and perhaps to answer – the question of what education is for. Centralised control of schools has never been greater and school leaders are to a very great extent reduced to agents of a state agenda. But some do ask the bigger questions. And while no school leader can afford to ignore the standards drive – and most would not want to – many want to work towards a larger vision. At the same time, requirements from the Government have become more open and schools that are bold enough can have greater freedoms to determine what they undertake with students.

With funding from the Calouste Gulbenkian Foundation, a number of secondary schools in England have joined the Human Scale Schools project, exploring human scale ideas that they believe can work for their students, their institutions and their circumstances. Most of the Human Scale Schools projects funded by the Foundation centre on Key Stage 3 students. All schools involved have different visions but share a commitment to growing stronger relationships in school, often partly through smaller communities.

Since 2006, 39 schools have received grants to develop human scale practice with their own staff and students. Some have changed their organisation within existing buildings and curriculum – creating mixed-age tutor groups at Didcot Girls' School in Oxfordshire for instance, to reduce bullying and enhance a sense of community.

Others have made more ambitious changes. In the final year of grants for the Human Scale Schools project, four schools – Brislington Enterprise College, Stantonbury Campus, Walker Technology College and Stanley Park High School – have been appointed as 'lead schools'.

Stantonbury Campus in Milton Keynes is building on a long tradition of innovative practice and school organisation; students belong to one of five Halls, mini-schools of around 500, and there is a campus ethos of 'equal value' and what principal Mark Wasserberg calls 'determined optimism about every student's potential'. In the last two years, Stantonbury has begun a programme of curriculum development at Key Stage 3. As part of this, students engage in Rich Tasks – themed, trans-disciplinary, project-based learning. In, for instance, 'Heroes and Villains – Creating a Campaign', work from art, drama, music, and the integrated English and humanities culminates in a collapsed timetable day in which students present their campaigns to visitors.

Stantonbury is working on developing alternative forms of assessment.

Walker Technology College sits in a loop of the Tyne, in an area once dominated by shipbuilding. People here have struggled to recover from the loss of traditional employment opportunities but are proud of their heritage and community. Walker students are loyal, open and friendly – but need a lot of support, says head teacher Steve Gater. 'We need to be very close to our students. We really are surrogate parents when it comes to giving advice and support.'

Although at the time of writing Walker is a national challenge school, it has historically fared well in exams. Dr Gater describes it as an 'educational foie gras factory', where students are stuffed with what they need to know. From 2011, when Walker moves into its new BSF premises, each student will be a member of one of three mini-schools, still named for the Victorian heroes of the area – builder Grainger, engineer Stephenson and architect Dobson. They will belong to a community that knows them, says Steve Gater. The aim is to empower students in their learning, and motivate them through closer relation-ships with fewer teachers and a more relevant curriculum, with Years 7 and 8 oriented around skills. 'Knowing kids inside out is the key to success, particularly here. What we want is a goose that *wants* to become bigger and better...'

Deputy head Mike Collier describes the aspiration that students should be 'charged by learning' and 'work savvy'. 'Do I care if they know all the dates of the major battles?' he asks. 'Not really'. He cares, he says, that they should know how to find out those dates. 'Once you've got those skills, the world's your oyster.'

Stanley Park High School in Wallington, Surrey, has invested in a Year 7 'block' – of flexible indoor and outdoor learning spaces, in which to provide an integrated curriculum. 'For us it is not just about their maths and their English. It's about their development as young people in a lot of other areas and that's not valued,' says deputy head Jacqui Thomas. Stanley Park leaders want to equip their students with confidence, skills and autonomy as well as exam passes.

American experience...

In the United States, with a longer and more widespread history of small schools, there are many convincingly successful models of small schools that have over years developed unique ways of working with their communities and students. Although often housed in dilapidated premises, they are characterized by visionary and courageous leaders, and all remain works in progress – places where staff and students work together to continue to evolve their thinking and practice, rather than arrive at a static status quo.

The Julia Richman education complex on Manhattan's Upper East Side was once an outsized high school and now houses six micro-institutions. One of them is the Urban Academy, with just 120 pupils – a 'transfer school' for students who have been unhappy or in trouble at other schools. The Academy takes up most of the second floor of the large utilitarian building, and shares library, canteen and sports facilities with the other schools on the Julia Richman site. Couches in the wide corridors, a students' coat stand, and black-and-white student photography on the walls all contribute to a homely informality.

With a small number of staff and students, the curricular range is limited. But following the human scale principle of 'less is more' students at the Academy go deep into fewer subjects. Learning is enquiry-based; small class sizes and secure relationships underpin the extensive debating and out-of-school work undertaken here. The names of courses – 'oh my God', 'talking about Cuba', 'about men and women', 'project adventure' – clearly signal their relevance to students' lives beyond school.

'Comprehensive schools can offer a great range of courses – but how many courses can kids take?' says Ann Cook, inspirational co-principal of the Urban Academy. 'We're a small school but we have a richer curriculum and offer more interesting ways of learning. How many kids leave school with a passion, an interest, a curiosity that they can hold on to, that connects them with the human experience? I think many schools are doing a pretty good job of turning kids off.'

Students and staff know each other well at Urban Academy; the intimacy of the relationships is obvious, as students move along the corridor and in and out of the communal office. 'Young people here can connect with adults. They see adults talking to each other, having fun, laughing,' says Ann Cook. Small scale, in itself, is not enough. 'It is a necessary but not sufficient pre-condition. You have to think about – what does small give you an opportunity to do? Change teaching, change timetabling, change space. It's about instruction.'

Almost all Urban Academy students go on to further or higher education.

growing up in England...

The Labour Government's investment in schools and focus on standards has improved exam results over the last ten years. Despite this, the proportion of young people leaving school with five good GCSEs is still only at 65 per cent, and fewer than half have five including maths and English. Too many children are still cast as failures by the system – and absorb that as the most profound lesson from their time in school.

Mike Davies, formerly head of the human scale Bishops Park College at Clacton, Essex, was motivated by this scenario to try and create a school that made success possible for all young people. 'The system privileges some,' he says. 'For others – their talents will never be recognised. I had an increasing sense of frustration, bordering on anger, that the National Curriculum legitimises certain forms of knowledge, while casting out others.'

Current Government moves towards apprenticeship and diplomas are aimed at addressing the needs of a wider range of students. But these still risk having second-class status within schools that are focused primarily on academic achievement.

Paper qualifications of whatever kind tell only part of the story. By broader measures – including the 2007 United Nations Children's Fund index of youth wellbeing – England's children are scoring alarmingly poorly.

UNICEF rated children's experience under six headings: material wellbeing, health and safety, family and peer relationships, educational wellbeing, behaviours and risks, and subjective wellbeing. The study involved 21 industrialised countries, including most of Europe plus Canada and the United States.

Children in the UK came bottom in the overall average ranking for 'wellbeing', with the USA scoring only fractionally higher. Bottom in 'family and peer relationships', and in the category 'behaviours and risks'. Bottom in 'subjective wellbeing' (where the children in the Netherlands scored most highly). And close to bottom in 'material wellbeing' and 'educational wellbeing'.

Educational wellbeing was measured through achievement at age 15 in reading, maths and science, the proportion of students remaining in education until the age of 18 and the proportion proceeding from school to employment or training.

children in the UK

An incessant stream of media stories backs up the UNICEF conclusion about the situation of children in the UK. A quarter of those surveyed for the Prince's Trust in 2008 said they were often or always 'down or depressed'. Half the adults interviewed by YouGov felt children were 'increasingly a danger to others'.

More than 65,000 students were temporarily excluded from schools for violence against other students in 2006/07, according to official data, an overall rise of more than 4 per cent on the previous year. Children's enjoyment of school decreases from Reception onwards, kids told CBBC's Newsround. Although 82 per cent of 6 to 8-year-olds enjoyed school, only 72 per cent of 9 to10-year-olds did and the percentage dropped to 67 for students aged 11 to12 years.

The Children's Society published in February 2009 a report called *A Good Childhood*, warning of the multiple pressures and disadvantages faced by children in the UK. On education, the authors highlighted the negative effects of too much testing. They commented: 'We recognise the importance of qualifications as one of the most significant outcomes of learning for children as they grow older, but we believe that exam grades and qualifications must not be seen as the primary objective of children's education, rather as one of the markers of children's growth, learning and achievements among many others… The Children's Society believes that the development of children's personal, social and emotional capabilities should be given the same priority as the development of cognitive capabilities in schooling.'

CHAPTER THREE
Lister's base rooms

Lister Community School is in Plaistow, east London, set beyond the point where the underground emerges above ground, in a landscape of low-rise social housing blocks, boarded-up pubs and betting shops. Inside the high school gates, Lister is a typically scruffy-looking English secondary, with a range of buildings dating from different educational eras. What they call here 'the new building' is ten years old but with its cracking walls and worn linoleum, appears worn out. The 'old building' by contrast – dating from the first half of the last century when Lister was a technical school – is a pleasant, brick construction around a grassy courtyard, netted overhead to keep out pigeons.

Lister is part of the Building Schools for the Future (BSF) programme, and if all goes according to plan will move into new premises in 2010. But staff at the school are redesigning practice in advance of the move. Thirty of this autumn's new Year 7s will join the second year of a pilot project designed to begin to turn this large school – of 1,350 students – into what the head teacher Martin Buck hopes will become a more intimate and meaningful learning community. 'I believe in human beings,' says Martin Buck. 'I want the sense that their potential can emerge.'

The experimental 'base room' project with new students attempts to create a network of close and secure relationships from the starting point of a tutor group that spends its time with a small number of teachers and mainly in one, well-equipped room.

learning at Lister...

Head teacher Martin Buck joined Lister in 1999, from headship in a Harrow school and following experience in a range of London boroughs. The students at Lister appealed to him, he says. 'They had an interesting quality; they were less cynical. Less worldly. That's more complex now.'

When Martin Buck arrived, this was the fourth most deprived borough in England. Now, it's risen to be the sixth but there remains a lot of underlying poverty in the backgrounds of Lister's students, who are mainly Muslim. Families want the best for their children – there is good attendance at learning review evenings – but the few middle class parents in the area tend to send their children over the borough border to schools in Redbridge.

Despite these factors, Lister is popular and consistently oversubscribed. Footballer Sol Campbell attended the school as did wheelchair basketball player Ade Adepitan – best known for his slot in the BBC2 logo. Performing arts – the school's specialism – has harnessed student enthusiasm, created success and is a big part of the school's identity. The school seems to succeed in helping its students find a positive way in to adult life. Few pupils from Lister – only 5 per cent – join the lost generation of 'NEETS' (a Government acronym for 'not in education, employment or training') after leaving school. An increasing proportion go on to university – often remaining in London and living at home while doing so. For Lister's Muslim girls, this can be a way of satisfying both personal aspirations and cultural requirements.

The white working class boys who are most at risk of school failure are in a small minority at Lister. But with many students combining in their lives two cultures, two languages and the strains of growing up in a deprived part of London, kids are 'particularly focused here', says Martin Buck. 'They need continuity, they need consistency. They need to believe in the people around them. Then they give a high level of trust. Any teacher here must have grit, relationship-building capacity, humour in modest amounts – kids don't want comedians – and passion for them to do their work. Then they can get results.'

Despite the fact that the school does well both in terms of GCSE passes and value-added scores, leadership here wanted to make changes. 'There may be more exam success,' says Martin Buck. 'But we know in our hearts that too few kids know how to learn. Too few understand, and are ready for, lifelong learning.'

Martin Buck expresses frustrations with the traditional school curriculum and organisation. 'We have a nineteenth-century design for a twenty-first-century agenda,' he says. 'The subject has been the dominant category of how we define teaching and learning, but the traditional design fragments relationships, or can do.' He and other senior staff are interested in moving the school towards a new form of pedagogy based at least partly on trans-disciplinary learning. 'We think now we can construct something that couldn't previously have happened,' says the head, describing the process as 'slow burn'.

'Teacher collaboration, student collaboration and deep learning, are the goals. We don't claim here at the moment that we've got into the totality of what human scale education stands for. Our model would be a hybrid. But we want strong relationships with fewer adults, who get to know young people in the round and have the ability to praise, reward, go through crises – and still come out with a learning agenda, because we're not social services.'

Plans for the new BSF building are underway; meanwhile, Lister has begun its change process by piloting a new experience for some of the Year 7 students. Historically, children at the school start well, says the head, but a fragmented first year experience of many different teachers and subjects leads to a dip in performance in Year 8. They wanted to introduce a transition curriculum in Year 7 that would help build confidence, foster positive relationships and assist students in becoming more effective learners.

They began two years ago to emulate a scheme they had observed in Norway – well-resourced 'base rooms' for Year 7 students, in which they remain for 45 per cent of the time, are taught intensively by a smaller than usual team of teachers and where the focus is on creating success through developing students' social and learning skills, and self-confidence.

The scheme was introduced as a pilot project at Lister with just one tutor group in the academic year 07/08, and continued with a second group in 08/09. It had and has the important added element of a film-maker working with the children on digital media, in a scheme sponsored by the National Endowment for Science, Technology and the Arts (NESTA). The NESTA project was designed to integrate information technology – in the form of digital media – across the curriculum and to test the effective of trans- and cross-curricular projects.

Last year, says head teacher Martin Buck, the pilot group in the base room benefited from the experience. 'Students did feel they could build relationships. They were more open with adults. Worked collaboratively. Became better listeners. We know that fewer faced fixed-term exclusions, and internal exclusions.'

However, some of the students felt constrained by staying in the base room, rather than moving around the school like their non-pilot-scheme Year 7 peers. 'Some were still critical of that experience. They knew they got the bonus of the film activities – but still felt frustrations.

the new base room students…

On a breezy overcast September day, the first of the new school year 2008, Year 7 gather for an assembly in Lister's old sports hall; children in barber-fresh haircuts and unscuffed black shoes sit in long lines under the wall bars. 'We have high expectations of you,' Martin Buck tells them from the podium in a clear, encompassing voice. 'Every one of you is going to find something that you love, something that you're good at. You're going to find your talent and we're going to help you grow your talent.' He encourages them to stay on for after-school clubs, whatever their required attendance at mosque or temple – or church, he adds, unflinchingly – may be.

As the Year 7s disperse for the first time to their new classrooms, 30 of them follow Ally Wiseman into a larger than average, ground floor space, with 15 new-looking Apple Macs – courtesy of NESTA – sitting on the workbenches around the edges of the room. This is the base room, where this year's pilot 7M students will belong. Students in the group will spend much of their time in this room and remain here for English, maths, humanities and PHSE.

Ally Wiseman is the form tutor for this second year of the pilot project. Ally, tall in patent stilettos, has an energetic, confident manner with both kids and colleagues. An English teacher, with only her qualifying year behind her, Ally didn't volunteer for the role but says she is keen to do it. 'I wasn't quite sure about it, but now I'm excited.' Assisted by learning support assistant Narinjan Rathore Singh – sturdy, with a diamond stud in his ear and a background in youth work – Ally will teach English to 7M and team-teach humanities with scheme co-ordinator Traci Clark and humanities teacher Susan Skyers.

The first priority is to begin to get to know the new students. Ally Wiseman plays a warm-up game with 7M, in which students say their name and add something they like and something they dislike. Hussein doesn't initially know what he dislikes. 'Aah', he remembers. 'Literacy'. And he is not alone. Maha is frightened of spiders, and Wazir hates Chelsea football team. But dislike of literacy and numeracy quickly emerges as one thing this group may have in common.

Ally tells 7M that their homework is to stick their new timetable in the front of their planners. Now, they must write down this instruction. Not all do. Hussein gets out his 'handwriting pen' – a product currently being advertised on television as adapted for either right- or left-handers – and makes a note in a tidy script. But Nathan, plump and puzzled-looking, struggles to write these few words.

By the end of the school day, a crowd of silent parents are gathered round the gates, their eyes trained anxiously on the children that stream towards them. If children fear transfer to 'big school', parents often fear it more.

lost in the middle…

Traci Clark, a humanities teacher, is the co-ordinator of the base room project at Lister. In its first year, she and the then 7M form tutor were with the students for half of their timetable. They team-taught humanities for four periods and she taught the group English and maths as well. 'At first, I thought I couldn't teach maths,' she says. 'But because it's not my subject, I could relate to the problems children had with it. It's been an eye-opener for me, that I can teach it. I take it down to the basics, they don't see it as very structured and all about book work.'

Traci Clark went into the base room with enthusiasm. 'I thought it was a great idea. I'm quite open to new ideas and I'd worked in learning support. What they said was – instead of coming in to thirteen teachers in secondary school, with a big drop in learning and behaviour, we could cut down the number of teachers, to about seven.'

The school held an open evening to explain the idea to parents; only ten parents attended but those who came responded positively. 'They liked the idea that there were key people,' says Traci, 'that their child wouldn't get lost in the system.'

The group was randomly selected and had an average mix of students with special needs, and the gifted and talented. 'It helped create a sense of solidity for students,' says Traci. 'There weren't any "lost in the middle". The ones that float along not really doing very much at all in normal classes – they were the ones we wanted to make a big push on, the middle ones who can go either way. We were able to focus on them. Usually, it takes two to three months to even get to know their names.'

A big part of the aim was to foster more positive relationships between students.

'We wanted them all to work with every single person in the group,' says Traci. 'That was a priority. Because by Year 9 they can be really mean to each other, show real animosity. We wanted to stop that. If antisocial behaviour isn't addressed now, it becomes problematic for their learning and it escalates.

'We encouraged the idea that they're looking out for each other and have to learn to work together, that even if they're not great friends, they can still co-operate. They all worked with everyone. They're really nice kids. I really like them as people. They're not nasty. Haven't got that meanness about them. At first, they were your typical Year 7s and didn't want to speak. We worked and worked

student voice

Tamina, a Year 8 student, has her arms still patterned with henna following the recent Muslim festival of Eid. Age 12, she is articulate and confident and was in the base room during Year 7.

'Before I came, I was a bit nervous about being in big school with those big students, and us being little. You feel you might get bullied, by older people, pushing you about and swearing at you and calling you names.

'When we came, they told us we'd be using the base room which had a lot more equipment, so we could do practical work, have fun and learn in a better way, a way that we could all get to know each other really quick. We were excited and I thought it was a good idea because if we're learning in a fun way then we learn a lot better and we enjoy learning more.

'We did practical work, like drama, role play, cutting and sticking; we used to do big posters, display work that went around the classroom. And we did a lot more talking in class and discussion work.

'We got to know everyone within about two or three weeks because we were in our base room so much and we were doing discussion work. We got to know the teachers quite good too. We had our two tutors, our English teacher, our humanities teacher and a couple of other teachers outside the base room. We still did go round the school and go to other rooms for different lessons. Sometimes we used to be in our base room a bit too much. But most of the time it was fun in there.

'In Year 8, it gets a bit boring now. I enjoy some of the subjects. I like PE, I like maths, and technology and art. And history as well. We kind of miss the base room because it was a lot more fun in there. We're still going to get to do our media projects. In Year 8, we're not allowed to talk in lessons. It's just written work.

and worked with that. The filming was key. They definitely became more confident.

'The kids who didn't like it were the very slow learners, who used to do very little, in a series of classes. In the base room, they had to finish their work. Because there was no lesson changeover, you gain quite a bit of time. And they had to finish things before moving on to the next thing. We found it suited the more needy children, the ones with special needs. It was consistent, they had their own trays. It was

'It was good for everyone, everyone who gets that opportunity can learn properly. For kids who aren't interested in school, they might enjoy it because there are more resources, like computers and everyone likes going on computers.'

Syeed, 12, was also in Lister's base room last year.

'First, when I heard about it, I thought 7M was going to be boring. I really wanted to go round the school for lessons. But as I got into it, I thought it was really fun.

'In the base room, because we used to be together a lot, we could build up trust. So you could tell them anything. Because we used to do group work, we would work together to get our work finished, and just trust each other, basically.

'Every Friday, we had something like circle time and anything that we had on our minds or we were upset about we could just tell them and it would stay in the circle. In the base room, we'd hang around together. But as soon as we got into Year 8, people thought – "oh, we're big now, we'll go and look for better friends, who are like us."

'I wouldn't want base room through my whole school life. It used to get boring sometimes and it used to get really hot as well. Maybe for one or two years but by Year 10 you can be independent and you don't need your teachers and friends no more.

'In 7M, they used to let you talk – say what your opinion was. Now in Year 8, it's just what teachers think, really. I prefer working in groups because you can discuss things and have a different opinion from each other. If you agree with one thing and someone else agrees with another thing, then they can tell you why they agree with it. Then you might understand what they mean.'

more linked to primary, not such a big jump, with less movement around the school.

'And it suited children who were terrified of coming to secondary school, it was good for them. We had more time, doing that nurturing side. And we had closer contact with the parents. They'd drop in, at period 5 to talk about homework or whatever. They knew we were there at the end of every day.'

One of the hopes for the base room group, says Traci Clark, was that it would improve attendance. Last year poor attenders came regularly on the days they were scheduled to spend the whole day in base room – but on the days when they had to join in with normal school life and move around the school like other students, their attendance slipped again.

A key aim of the project is to make transition smoother so that students don't switch off school. 'We don't want them to lose all that enthusiasm,' says Traci Clark. 'We wanted to make them into confident kids, with high self-esteem. Independent learners, with very high confidence, because when you speak to kids the thing that comes out all the time is the frustration that they can't learn in a certain way. You have to find another way in.'

The first year of the pilot group was not formally evaluated. But the impact of having a limited number of teachers, a secure base and a culture of working together is evident in the now Year 8 group, she says, who have fewer problems than any other group in the same year. 'They are respectful. They can be quite chatty. But they're enthusiastic and keen. They all have their own learning styles. They've developed autonomy. They don't need every little instruction given to them. They can get on with things. And they'll come up with something you didn't think of, as a teacher. They'll be original, if you'll let them.'

'Hopefully by Year 9 they will have a clear idea of what they can do, what they can achieve…'

changing and learning…

A week into the autumn term, Ally Wiseman wants to get the new 7M to begin to think about themselves as learners. She tells them about a time she didn't enjoy learning – doing a long comprehension, while her teacher read a magazine – and a time when she did – 'with my German teacher, who was an absolute nutter. But who made my lessons fun. We didn't have to sit there in silence all the time.'

The students have to think of a time when they did, and did not, enjoy their learning. When did small, bespectacled Omar enjoy his learning? She has to press him for an answer. 'I never have. Because it's all boring. There's no life to it.' What did he like about primary school, Ally persists. School trips, he ventures in the end. Mohamed says he hated Year 6 maths – because the teacher got angry very quickly. 'And if one person did something wrong, we'd all get punished.' Charmaine says she liked it when her class used to go to the park.

Next, Ally Wiseman gets the class to draw their positive and negative experiences of school. Samira's 'negative' is of children sitting in rows, on chairs. It represents, she says, 'the teacher going on and on and on'. Sukey's 'positive' is her favourite teacher, drawn in her combat trousers and flowery T-shirt and with a smiling face. It is instructive to see the negatives – boards covered in numbers, teachers who shout, who constantly test... And the positives: those who make things with them, laugh, help. 'It's time to make Easter baskits,' one teacher's speech bubble announces.

Nathan starts to write rather than draw because, he says, 'I'm a bad drawer'. Then he remembers he can't write easily either, and fiercely rubs out the start he has made. What did he like about learning? 'Doing literacy on the computer instead of in a book.' What did he dislike? 'When my teacher shouted at me.'

Ally Wiseman introduces the component parts of ELLI (Effective Lifelong Learning Inventory) – the skills-based learning that is a key aspect of the transition curriculum. On the board, projected from the computer, are what she calls seven ways of learning.

Changing and learning
Meaning making
Critical curiosity
Creativity
Learning relationships
Strategic awareness
Resilience

It is a challenge to introduce these unfamiliar concepts to 11-year-olds. When 7M students have to talk in groups about what they mean, silence falls, initially. But they are willing to try. 'Grow up and learn differently', Sukey writes by 'changing and learning'. 'Being curious about things and asking questions', someone else offers for 'critical curiosity'. 'Eager to learn', suggests Oliver.

Getting students to think about these ideas is part of the bid to give them greater awareness of themselves and their learning processes, to put them in charge of their learning and social selves, now and in the future. 'If we can become better at each of these skills then we can become better at learning,' promises the handout that accompanies the session.

base room's project days…

Part of the special school diet of 7M is a day per week spent entirely in the base room on themed humanities work taught through projects and bringing in the use of digital media, with the NESTA film-maker. The first theme is Identity, and on 7M's first project day Traci Clark tells the students that they will be working in groups, determined by the teachers, and that different groups will be doing different activities.

One group will begin with shoeboxes that they cover with fabric and pictures then fill with items or pictures that represent who they are. They can put in it, Traci says, a poem they wrote as a child, a ballet shoe, a certificate. 'Anything that is part of who you are, as a person.' Another group will be making self-portraits, using digital cameras to photograph themselves and then drawing from the prints. Another group will be assembling dolly figures – collages of themselves. And a fourth group will construct silhouettes of their heads.

They drag their tables – as instructed – into a horseshoe shape, and Traci gives out the resources. Amira, in a black headscarf and tunic, high fives her friend; she has found a shimmery length of turquoise gauze with which to cover her shoebox.

Working together is a major part of the intended learning. 'We will keep swapping you around so eventually you work with everyone,' Traci says. 'Put your hand up if you know what it means to work in a group.' The students seem cheerful and already integrated, in some imperceptible way. The ones who struggle with basic literacy – mainly, two boys – are busy with their work, encouraged by Narinjan Singh. The push to help young students get on with each other, to feel and show respect for each other, is always important but clearly so in a classroom like this one – where children's cultural heritages include Yemeni, Jordanian, Palestinian, Pakistani, Bengali, Indian, Traveller, Afro-Caribbean, Somali, white British and Polish.

Exploration of the theme of Identity is occurring naturally, as students get to know each other and themselves in this new context. 'Are you a Muslim?' one boy asks the girl sitting next to him. 'No,' she says coolly. 'I believe in science.' What does gentle-seeming Charmaine think of project day: 'Pretty. Lovely. Nice.' In the silhouette of her own head, she sticks pictures of pink things – a pair of Uggs, a necklace, a stuffed toy. Charmaine usually sticks close to the friend she came with from primary school but today is on a different table from her.

student voice

Priya, 11, is one of the new base room students at Lister.

'Base room is like your place where you kind of belong. For English, maths and humanities – we're in base room. We don't have to remember a lot of rooms – we can just go there. We don't have to remember a lot of different rules.

'When you're in the base room, you're used to hanging around with the people that are in your class. In every lesson we sit with different people, so then you get to know them. It's actually quite nice because sitting with the same people is a bit dull. Different people have different feelings and they tend to have a different attitude so that's quite interesting as well.

'All my teachers I kind of like. I guess I've got to know them a bit more so I'm not as stiff as I was before. Project day – I enjoy it a lot, because there's different activities and every time you finish something, there's something else.

'In primary school, it was normally the teachers planning everything for us. On project days, yes – they're planning bits for us. But most of the time we're doing it on our own.

'It feels as if they've given you responsibility and independence so you can do it all yourself.'

Nathan, who is a potential candidate for Lister's nurture group, searches through a pile of tabloids for a Manchester United photo to put in his Identity shoebox. Learning assistant Narinjan has formed a close relationship with Nathan and lobbied for him to stay in the mainstream group, where he is working very hard. It would have 'broken him', he says, to be transferred.

The students' enjoyment of what they are doing is clear. By break time, Traci Clark has to insist that they leave the room for a while. 'I know some of you have said you want to stay in but you need to get some fresh air. I don't want anyone staying in to do work – you're going to be in here for five hours today.' 'Yesssss', says one.

At the end of the morning session, they review the film that NESTA film-maker Yurena Asensio de Dios has shot of the session, seeing themselves talking, cutting things out, moving around the room. 'It's to show you what you are doing,' says Traci Clark. 'And to help you improve as a team member.'

Part of the drive in the base room is towards the most challenging form of knowledge – self-knowledge.

Identity exhibition...

Soon after half term, on the drizzly morning of a November day that seems as if it will not get light, Traci Clark introduces to 7M the prospect of an exhibition. 'The idea is for you to take control of it and present your work to the people that are coming in,' she tells the class. 'It's two weeks off and we're going to be doing it on Identity. Every single person will get the opportunity to say something. Because it's about you; the main part of the exhibition is to show off how brilliant you are.'

All their work on Identity will be on display, she tells them, and they will make presentations. One or two people on each table will be the main spokespeople. The audience will be a visiting class of Year 6s and their teacher. Later, some Year 10 Lister students will visit too.

'I like the base room because...' In preparation for the exhibition, Ally Wiseman solicits endings to this sentence. The students work in groups but all come up with their own contributions. It seems clear that they really do like the base room, and it is striking how clearly they express the feeling of belonging to the group.

Responses to 'I like the base room because...' include:

We all work together as a family
Do lots of projects
Lots of facilities
Get a lot of help
We get to work independently without the teachers there by our side
     every second
Room to move around
It's colourful and bright
So many electronics
We get good education and we trust each other like a family
It's very welcoming
We do fun activities
We get to explore ideas
Everybody helps me and they're like my friends
We can be creative and have ideas
We're very lucky because we work with Miss Yurena on Apple Macs

The responses are genuine and 7M are going to speak them to a visiting class of primary children. From being strangers a few weeks ago, they must now pull together. Traci Clark conducts the rehearsal. All are present. Oliver is one of the spokesmen, science-trusting Priya the other. 'Welcome to our Identity exhibition,' they chorus. Oliver continues. The shoebox, he says, showed them how identity is made up of lots of different elements.

Yurena Asensio de Dios films the rehearsal; before lunch, 7M watch themselves on the whiteboard and see how fidgeting, staring at the floor and folded arms don't show them at their best. Having reviewed the film together and been invited to make constructive comments on each others' performance, they have another go. By the third run through, most have got the hang of speaking loudly, slowly and clearly to an anticipated audience.

Only Hussein can't muster any enthusiasm for expressing what he feels about the base room. 'Don't you want to say it?' Traci asks. 'Because we don't want to make you say something you don't mean.'

At break, as all the others stream out to the playground, she keeps him back for a minute. 'Is it something personal?' He nods. 'You don't have to tell us what it is but don't bring it in to school and take it out on other people.'

The day of the exhibition has arrived and 7M are excited. A buzz fills the room. The Identity shoeboxes are arranged all along the bench on one side of the room. The half photo/half drawing self-portraits are up on the wall, and a notice on the door announces that '7M welcome you to our Identity exhibition'.

Once they have as a group made their spoken presentation, they will be demonstrating the practical work at their tables, with heaps of coloured felts, scraps of materials, glues, old magazines, scissors, lace, glitter and false hair to work with, according to which activity they are on. Different tables are demonstrating the four different Identity project activities: silhouette, shoebox, self-portraits and dolly figures. They can call them 'identity figures', says Traci, if they are averse to the word 'dolly'.

They run through the presentations one last time and have just got back into base room after morning break when their visitors arrive. Once the Year 6s are settled on the floor, Oliver and Priya introduce the Identity exhibition. Ally Wiseman stands listening, visibly proud. Once the presentations are over, the visitors swarm around the activity tables, open up the Identity shoeboxes and greet children they already know. The boys find their way to the Apple Mac computers and one of the visiting teaching assistants begins to make a dolly figure, with enthusiasm. The class teacher confirms that Year 6 like what they are seeing of secondary school. 'They're all coming up to me asking "can we do the same thing?"' she says. 'But it will have to wait till after SATs.'

Hussein gets overexcited and seems in danger of attracting Ally Wiseman's wrath. 7M's still-fragile maturity is grown and stretched by this multi-skilled activity. Year 6 again take up their sitting position and 7M stand in front of them, taking questions about big school.

Year 10 visit once Year 6 leave. The students – from Ally Wiseman's English GCSE class – show an enthusiastic interest in the work, looking in the Identity shoeboxes and asking questions. They seem intuitively to understand what they are seeing. 'I like this style of learning,' one Year 10 girl comments, as the group leaves. 'I wish we'd had it. Even the shy ones who don't talk – they're talking. I think the work has brought them together.'

7M's transition…

After one full term in the base room with 7M, form tutor Ally Wiseman feels she has more of a grip on the ideas and practice. 'What's become very clear,' she says, 'is that it is great for low-ability students and those with behavioural difficulties.' Nathan, for instance, not only struggles with reading and writing but even at primary school frequently got into violent fights. He was worried from the start that this would happen at secondary – but he hasn't been in any fights. 'He has behaved brilliantly,' says Ally. 'But part of that is because he has been in the base room.' His strong and supportive relationship with learning support assistant Narinjan seems to have helped his confidence and despite very poor literacy skills he has stayed with the group.

Socially, says Ally Wiseman, the class has gelled unusually well. 'I would have expected more spats and infighting among the girls, because they're getting to that age. But they are a very sound group.'

The experience hasn't been right for everyone. For the one 7M student who is withdrawn to attend Lister's nurture group for large chunks of time, the base room is not working. Because the rest of the group is so close and well-integrated, he struggles to fit in when he comes back to the class. 'He hates the base room,' says Ally. 'And he hates the nurture group as well.'

For Ally, it is the first time she has spent so much time with one group of students, being their tutor and teaching them English, PHSE and project. By Wednesday lunchtimes, she says, she has already been with them for five periods. 'I feel very close to them. I know all of them individually, know more about them even than my Year 10s. I feel protective and I think it means that I know how to handle them better, as a group. I can plan for them better, I know what interests them, what makes them tick.'

'They think I'm often strict but they don't just see us as teachers – they see us as people too. That's my sign that I'm doing the right thing. And if something's wrong, they come and tell me. I've had loads of Christmas cards from them. I think we're very close.'

Base room co-ordinator Traci Clark is doing what many teachers are unwilling to do – teaching almost across the curriculum in Year 7, in humanities, maths and English. Primary trained, she says it comes easily to her – although there are practical issues relating to her faculty identity, attendance at meetings and professional development sessions. 'Some people don't want to teach outside their comfort zone. They don't see the point. You've really got to be committed – otherwise it doesn't work. I think they could get more primary teachers involved. That would be something I'd recommend.'

Traci is pleased with the way 7M have begun their school lives. There have been no fixed-term exclusions or serious sanctions yet for the group, she says, and she feels this positive start will fuel them through a positive Year 8. 'We try to resolve behaviour rather than sanction it,' Traci says. 'We'll listen to problems. We don't often do structured lessons. It tends to be discussion and group work. We'll finish off with kids what they've started, rather than go on to something new. They come away with a thorough understanding.'

She tries to communicate with parents and carers and involve them in their children's progress. She has frequent text exchanges with the deaf mother of one of the students and talks to excitable Hussein's mother on the phone.

Part of the aim of the base room with its digital media resources is that it should prepare students to enrol for the Creative Media diploma introduced this year at Lister. This year's 7M will continue with media projects in Year 8, after they have left the base room. Last year's 7M, now in Year 8, are enthusiastic about their media work. Of the 30 students in the group, eight have told Traci Clark they plan to do the Diploma when they reach Year 10.

She stays in the base room thinking about the kids, long after they have gone home. Then pulls down the metal window shutters on the roomful of Apple Macs – five were stolen last summer, during the holidays – and locks the door.

The base room experience at Lister – in the academic year 09/10 – will extend to three tutor groups. In the new BSF school building, the intention is that all Year 7s will have this kind of experience.

CHAPTER FOUR
Brislington's new beginning

It is September 2008 and in the airy spaciousness that is the entrance to the new school, head teacher John Matthews welcomes students, requesting them to remove their outdoor jackets as they pass into the indoor/outdoor hybrid of the 'street'. The architects' drawings are finally animated, the big swathes of imagined colour manifest on the walls and windows of the five mini-school communities that have now taken physical form at Brislington. Students appear lively, excited and interested as they throng through the building in black-and-white uniforms. It is the first day on which the whole school has been present.

General announcements boom through the public address system – about a teacher's missing memory stick, students who haven't yet come to the office to be photographed for their ID cards. From further away, on the far side of the blue hoardings, the sounds of hammering and bulldozing continue – now coming from the demolition of the old school on what will become playing fields and open spaces. Here in the new building a parallel process of deconstruction must continue, if real culture change is to be achieved.

Panther community… for years 7 and 8

Autonomous mini-schools require autonomous mini-heads. Heather Evans, acting joint director of community for Panther, is sharing the role with Andy Cooper in this first term. Induction week went brilliantly she says, culminating in a 'Panther's Got Talent' day when the new Year 7s in the community performed for each other. Adults enjoyed it too; three colleagues came and hugged her at the end of the week, saying how glad they were to be part of it.

Panther – signature colour orange – is one of two communities for Year 7 and 8 students. The 182 student members of Panther have orange lockers, orange bands (here called lanyards) round their necks, for the ID/swipe cards that enable them to buy food, that open the door to their own quiet garden and that badge them with their house identity.

But the sense of identity is intended to go much deeper than a branding exercise. With fewer than 200 children in Panther, all the students should soon know each other and the 20 or so adults based in the community. New students in the junior communities will see only around eight teachers – humanities more than anyone – plus their learning guide. This is half the number they would have seen in the past.

The physical properties of the communities have been designed to foster intimacy. Panther, like all the five mainstream communities, is a bit like a two-storey 'house', situated on the school street. The director of community has a small office by the entrance with a large window facing out on to the street, and a glass panel in the door facing in to the community. It makes the director highly visible – and means they can see who comes in and out of the community, at least while they are in the office.

Community adults have an upstairs workbase from which they can look out on the school street. Classrooms are off a central hall that widens at the back to a social space just for Panther students, with an electronically controlled door to their semi-enclosed outdoor quiet space, visible through the plate glass. There are soft chairs in the social space and a printer; this public and unprotected siting of the printers sends a message to the students about community – about the need to behave responsibly, and not damage something that everyone needs.

The classrooms are carpeted, light-filled and the furniture easy to move around. The houses are high tech. Each community has 30 laptops and 30 'tablets' – the smaller version. Each classroom has a projector. There are several whiteboards. Teachers can send PowerPoint presentations to the classroom from their upstairs workbases. Some teachers are struggling both with the new methodology and with the new technology. ICT teething troubles are adding to the stress. 'I'm absolutely fed up,' breathes a senior teacher, exiting the workbase.

Lavatories for girls and women – they decided on a compromise in the end, with unisex loos on the main street and single sex ones within the communities – are opposite the director of community's office, and with no door on the entrance to the row of cubicles provide no opportunity for bullying or smoking – or, it might be added, for a female teacher to have a quiet moment. For school lavatories, these are exceptional, with clean modern basins, large mirrors and plentiful paper towels. The male lavatories are up the stairs.

Out on the street, the sandwich bars – in the style of high street coffee shops – send another message to the students that they are responsible; space has been made for them to socialise with each other in public, alongside their teachers and in full view of any visitors to the school. Students are on staggered breaks, with not more than 380 young people out at any one time.

building community...

Staff know that the building alone will not change things for Brislington students. Their task now is to create stronger relationships with students and with each other and continue to develop what happens in and out of the classroom.

Learning families are one of the building blocks of the new vision. Every adult working at Brislington will be 'learning guide' to a group of ten children. The new non-teacher learning guides – some of whom are apprehensive about the role – are mainly pairing up with teachers in the same community, and running sessions jointly. Learning guides have to monitor students' attendance, and behaviour, checking on e-portal whether any of their students have attracted either merits or sanctions, as indicated by a lightning icon by the name. They need to take electronic registers, learning the complex codes – there are 24 of them – issued by the DCSF to denote different forms of absence, and make time to talk to individual students about their targets. As well as these official and technical requirements, they are meant to be the person in school who really understands the student – socially, emotionally and in terms of their learning.

Andy Cooper, acting co-director with Heather Evans of Panther community, believes the learning families will have an impact. 'There are concerns, about people getting to grips with the role, but it is up to the directors of community to help them along. I definitely think that if you know a student better, you're going to be better able to serve their needs. It's spotting correlations, links. You might suddenly realise that a student has a really low attention span. You'll tune in to a student better. I firmly believe everyone is destined to be great at something.'

Despite the optimism brought about by the new building, Heather Evans and Andy Cooper know that to meet the nationally determined targets this community has an uphill struggle. Almost half of the incoming Year 7s are level 4C or below in English – a concern-causing level. Heather already has a list of the 27 children (including fifteen in academic support) whose literacy is very weak, plus another fifteen who need extra – but less intensive – support. The children in academic support include one boy who is an elective mute, a child with Asperger's, and others with speech problems, and depression.

student voice

Sadie, 11, has enjoyed her first week at Brislington, in Panther community.

'My dad gave me the choice, and I thought I should come here because it is local and my brother used to be here. I was worried about being bullied. Out of ten, I'm like a number nine, being worried about bullying. The older kids, sometimes they point at you and start talking with their friends.

'I've made quite a lot of new friends but sometimes I forget their names. I can't really say "Hi *Name*" – because I've forgotten it. I've enjoyed the PE lessons and having the cafeteria with baguettes, and these fruit juices. The card thing is really good because at primary school you had to bring in a pocket of money. Now you can just pop the money on your card.

'I've got one question. If we're in Panther, why are all the rooms white? Why can't they all be orange? Because it would show that your classroom is part of Panther. The building is really good. It's a nice change, to have mixed loos and it's good that the walls go up to the ceiling and down to the floor because in our junior school it was a bit low, so people could look over.

'I like the disabled children being here too. It shows they can handle all types.

'From outside it looks like just a plain old school but when you walk in you're overflowed with all these nice things. People are welcoming you and teachers sometimes just let you have a talk with

Andy Cooper's key word for his aspirations here? 'Belonging. I want them to feel that they can always come back to that community and there will be somebody who'll talk to them. That it's a kind of home, really.'

Key Stage 4...

Years 9, 10 and 11 students have gone into the senior communities, Jaguar and Puma. Simon Burrows, at Brislington since 1994 and a former head of year and assistant head, is director of community of Jaguar, the green-themed community of 317 students.

'I feel it's all but a headship. I need to be more strategic than I needed to be as head of year. John is still the head but has to invest them. They give you a chance when it's not in front of the whole class. You have your own locker as well.'

Errol, 11, was impressed by the £30 million he heard they were spending on the school.

'It's a brand new school, they've got all the technology and key cards and the idea of the communities, to stop bullying and stuff. We just spent ages becoming top of the school. Then it's back to the bottom of the heap. I thought big school would be bad, when I was in Year 4, but now they've brought in all this community stuff, I feel a lot safer around the school.

'The thing I like is that they've got a bit of a range of different food. The thing I don't like is that it's all healthy stuff. I think they could maybe sell a few doughnuts or something.

'My favourite subject is science. I'm really hands on. I like to mix different chemicals together to make stronger reactions. At primary school it was all just writing in the books. Pretty boring really. All we did was mix vinegar with bicarbonate of soda. Our teacher did it, it went everywhere, she had to take it to the sink.

'I saw some posters, showing kids pouring stuff into test tubes. I've had one lesson in science, here. Learning to use the Bunsen burner. It was fun. You had to change it from blue to yellow. Three lessons a day is much better because you learn more about it. In our old school, just as you were getting to the good stuff, the bell went.

'But long lessons could get a bit boring. After a bit, you get tired of concentrating. Then you get detention.'

complete trust in the heads of community – and he has said he will. We have been used to running our ideas past him.

'In the past, there has been a number of students who slip through the net. Not the academic, and not the most disaffected. A chunk of "lost" students, in the middle. I now should be able to know all 300 students. And I expect the learning guides to know students backwards. I believe we'll have a greater rapport with our students. When I was at school, I was much more likely to achieve, if someone knew me.'

Senior students at Brislington can from Year 10 enter one of five Pathways, ranging from the most academic, intended to lead on to A-levels and higher education, to the most vocational – which includes

student voice

Brislington's Year 11 students, unless they stay on for post-16, will have just one year of the new school experience.

Sasha, 16, is cautiously impressed. 'I like it. It's very light and bright. But it's hard for us to get used to it. We're in the same boat as the Year 7s, not knowing our way around. I like all the windows.

'Communities make it more kind of personal. Like, "that's my learning guide up there." Teachers can get to know you better, know what you should be achieving. The only problem is – no one knows where they're going. And our teachers don't have our books. We have to have them in our lockers.'

Kit, also 16, likes the new, longer, lessons. 'The old school was falling apart. The walls were falling apart and all the tables had graffiti on them and chewing gum stuck to them.

'The way they brought us in was organised. But I don't like it much, compared to the old school. It seems odd to me. We're split up into community breaks. You don't get to see some of your friends. Communities are a good idea – but it could have been done in friendship groups. Although you are making new friendship groups.

'I much prefer having three lessons a day. My day seems much quicker and a lot more does get done in the lessons. In some ways it's quite weird. You're used to seeing lots of teachers and now you're seeing fewer. If you get on well with your teacher, you learn a lot better. But if you don't get on well with the teacher, there's this feeling that they're picking on you, or they think you're just messing around in their lesson. With coursework, you need to be able to talk to your teacher.

'I can always tell if a teacher likes me or not. They won't tell you off so much. In some ways, it's quite unfair for a teacher to like some more than others.'

college and workplace experience and is intended to lead to post-16 GNVQ courses and then employment.

The options are still changing; last year, only one per cent of students got a good GCSE pass in a language, once students had the option to drop modern foreign languages. They are looking at introducing a BTec qualification in languages.

'Some need other curricula,' says John Matthews. 'They need a broad range on offer.' Two students, for instance, who have had eighteen months of 'appropriate courses' are now almost 100 per cent attenders, having been frequently absent when their school diet was of non-stop failure. 'They want to gain success,' says the head.

100-minute lesson…

One of the most controversial changes in the new school is the move to divide the day into three 100-minute lessons. The leadership team believe it will encourage deep engagement, in place of what Janine Foale terms 'lily pad learning'. Staff – some at least – felt it was too long a time to ask children to concentrate, especially for the lower sets.

Upstairs in Panther community, Rebecca Rowe is teaching her first 100-minute lesson – on 'poetic terms and devices' – in a pleasant, carpeted, classroom, to a group of Year 8s. Students are put in sets in English from Year 8 and this is a top set.

There is a rapid-fire session on assonance, similes, rhyme, rhythm and onomatopoeia. She shows them how to clap syllables, how to feel them – by putting a hand under the chin. 'I want to hear some talking,' Mrs Rowe calls out, then takes the register while they are working.

She moves on to a game of literary Bingo; students have to match the poetic terms they have written into their nine-space cards with the definitions she reads out. When a couple have shouted out the magic word, she asks the class for a show of hands on how well they have understood what has been covered so far. Hands closed means confused or lost, hands spread means 'really easy'. 'Don't panic,' she says, to the two who give her the closed hand sign. 'We will get you up to speed.' Not understanding is cast as the teacher's failure, not the student's.

She explains why she wants to hear voices. 'Why does it make our learning better, when we talk?' And with the students arrives at the answer. 'We're forced to start putting our thoughts into words. By trying to get it out, we can start thinking a bit more clearly.'

It's a fast-paced lesson. The classroom is light, with huge windows, their top panels in Panther's hallmark orange. The carpeted floor softens the sound. Mrs Rowe sets an encouraging tone; no one's contribution is disparaged. When a boy talks to his friend while a girl is speaking to the class, he has to apologise to her.

Rebecca Rowe makes Chaucer approachable. What might they do to entertain themselves, if they were riding from Bristol to Canterbury?

'Cook. Play I-Spy. Get plastered. Poke each other with sticks. Sing.' All answers make their way on to the board.

Subject boundaries have been redefined at Brislington, with faculties merged to form new areas of Experience. Science, and design and technology (DT) have come together to form Discovery. Humanities replaces history, geography and RE. 'Eurotime' is modern foreign languages, expanded to include the study of countries. Enterprise – the school's specialism – is made up of ICT and business studies. PE keeps its name. Dance, drama, music and art will be rotated term by term in students' timetables and with English make up a new area of Experience called Creative.

The intention is for Years 7 and 8 to have project-based lessons, with common themes running through the different areas of Experience. There are six themes in the course of Year 7, another six in the course of Year 8, decided on by heads of faculties – now called directors of experience.

This is 33-year-old Rebecca's fifth year of teaching; she is assistant director of experience, in the newly formed Creative faculty (which encompasses English, sport, music, art, dance and drama). This lesson – the second of the day – has a 20-minute break in the middle of it and, on duty in the quiet garden, a small landscaped space with topiary and benches, she talks about her new role in Panther community.

'Last year, everyone was quite negative about teaching Years 7 and 8, not 9, 10 and 11. But I went to a middle school myself and quite a few of us now are thinking it wouldn't be so bad to commit to teaching Years 7 and 8 for a time.' Because it's non-exam-focused, it's dynamic. You can be so creative, because it's not curriculum-focused. You can do things you couldn't do with other year groups.'

She is not entirely convinced about the longer lessons. 'I need more rationale, about why we're doing the 100-minute lessons,' she says. 'They don't bother me – but I need to see how the students are doing, because it's a long time for them to maintain concentration.'

After break, students are asked to translate a part of the *Pardoner's Tale*. They read – with a limited glossary – Chaucer's descriptions of the Miller, the Pardoner, the Prioress, the Knight and the Wife of Bath – then match pictures of each to the verse describing them. It's a quest and it's fun. 'Middle English is very different,' Mrs Rowe encourages them, 'but if you read it out loud – it's not so different.'

student voice

Alex, from Year 10, is in Jane Graydon's learning family. 'Families' meet every day at the end of school, for 20 minutes.

'In the old school, the toilets were dirty and there was vandalism – smashing windows with footballs, drawing on the walls. I didn't have a clue where anything was. But I got used to it after a week or so.

'Here, I like how new it is, and the design. As soon as you start – you're not wandering about the entire school. You don't get lost as much or as badly. Before, you had to go from one building to another.

'I used to have a very bad temper. When people kept going on, sometimes I just lost it. I'd kick chairs. Swear. I grew out of it. I thought – what's the point? I still get annoyed by people, but I just try to ignore it.

'My learning guide's nice. She's one of these people that help you, in school. I like reading. I like Harry Potter. They're the only books I've really read.'

For the last part of the lesson, they must devise their own character going on a journey and answer the same questions she put to them about a picture of a group of pilgrims, at the start of the lesson: Who are they? Where are they going? Why? What kind of story might they be telling?

Broken up into several different activities, with plenty of opportunity for group work and discussion, 100 minutes has passed painlessly and enjoyably.

Inevitably, not all lessons pass off so well. Upstairs, in one of the senior communities, a newly qualified teacher is teaching maths to a Year 10 set, and begins by giving them instructions on how to get started on their laptops in the MyMaths programme. The log-ins of the Dell laptops are slow, 'taking ten years' says one girl. It is the NQT's first lesson with this next-to-bottom set. There are only thirteen of them. But the muddle with the laptops – some will log on, some won't – means that the 100 minutes get off to a shambolic start. A couple of the boys begin to watch football matches online and tinny cheering fills the room.

teaching and learning...

Ina Goldberg is director of Cougar, the blue-themed Years 7 and 8 community at the far end of the street, next to the canteen area. Brislington has a longstanding arrangement with the University of the West of England (UWE), whereby teachers can accrue credits towards masters degrees. Ina Goldberg finished hers three years ago and is now studying for a PhD through UWE. Her research subject is 'learning relationships in small communities' and her interest in the developing practice here is unmistakeable. She has strong ideas – partly informed by her own education as a child in East Germany – but aims to harness other peoples' creativity too.

'I don't want to lead a community where the ideas come from only a handful of people,' she says. 'I want our community to be a place where kids enjoy what they're doing, and get the help they need when they need it. I want them to come to school, enjoy themselves, feel safe and feel they made the right choice to come here. And the same for the teachers. It'll be a big learning experience for everyone.'

Ina Goldberg says that in these first few days of the launch of the new school teachers are peculiarly disempowered, finding themselves facing some of the same challenges as new students. 'Students – they come to school to learn. But the way the school is being run means that teachers need to have a steeper learning curve than students. In a funny way, the students know what they are doing. But we don't. We have to change the way we teach, learn how to run the community. It's almost like the kids are more empowered than the teachers at the moment, because they know what they're doing.'

This is arguably how it should be, since real change is the desired outcome at Brislington. The creation of an altered school culture is a complex, time-consuming and uncertain process. There are principles – but no blueprint. 'Different schools will invent different ways to establish their unique culture – often diametrically opposite ways – as well as make their unique mistakes,' comments Deborah Meier, in *In Schools We Trust*.

Ina Goldberg sees her role as focused on teaching and learning. Most of the Cougar teachers are quite young – NQTs and people who've been in teaching three or four years. 'Enthusiastic, wanting to get on with the job. Creative. When I saw the list, I was really pleased,' she says. She runs coaching for Cougar teachers, and they can observe one another; one hour per fortnight is timetabled for peer observation. 'The whole idea is that people share ideas and teaching practice, that

Cougar's structure

There are 21 adults and 214 children in Cougar community. Of the adults, ten are teachers, one is a dedicated clerical support person and the others learning support assistants and a learning mentor. Four of the teachers are based in faculties outside the community – in PE, music and DT. The others are based in the community, and teach in Cougar for the majority of their time.

Support for students within the community is provided by a special educational needs co-ordinator, a community learning mentor and two learning support assistants. Cougar has a part-time community link person – whose role is to improve relations with students' families and the local area – who is also a part-time teacher. All the adults meet every morning at 8.30, to run through community matters, and again at the end of the day to discuss any issues arising. Even if they don't teach them, they need to know the students in the house.

The student members of Cougar consist of four Year 7 groups – each of about 30 students, three Year 8 groups, plus fifteen students with special needs. There is a Year 7 accelerated group – 7A1 – made up of those who got mainly level 5s in their SATs. All the other groups are mixed. Year 8s are put in sets according to ability, for English.

they actually have professional conversations. I don't think any teacher can say they are perfect. You can always learn something,' says Ina.

Students will have a core group of maths, English, Discovery, and humanities teachers. 'The idea is that they don't have to run to different places all the time, they belong to an area and they get to know a core group of teachers, so their transition process is much quicker,' says Ina. 'They get to know routines and faces and expectations. Staff learn their names more quickly. It should be that they have 50–60 per cent of their time with the same, community teachers.'

In this new Year 7, 50 per cent are at level 4C or below, in literacy. 'That's why problems start,' says Ina Goldberg. 'Because they can't access the traditional curriculum, they start with the behaviour issues, or they drop out – either mentally or literally – because they can't cope. And they don't have the support at home.

'A lot have other talents that are never looked at. And then they feel like failures. The impact is much greater in Years 9, 10, 11. We can be more flexible. We've got that time.'

John Matthews...

Upstairs, above the student entrance, the leadership team's office is orderly, with new peace lilies in china plant holders. The management volumes – *Good to Great, Just Do It, Destructive Emotions* – are neatly lined up on new bookshelves and the second hand on the 'Nice Day' wall clock jerks around the circuit. Deputy head Ruth Taylor has swapped her elegant heels for trainers; she has been teaching dance to a group of boys.

On the table lies a pile of cuttings, from the local paper the *Evening Post, The TES, Building Weekly*. Press comment so far has been favourable. There is a photograph of John Matthews walking down the now-famous street, with schools minister Jim Knight. Mr Knight's parting remark was: would they now be able to attain the required standards?

'All they're interested in is the 5 A*–Cs including maths and English,' John says. 'Nothing else.'

The first full day has gone smoothly. John remarks on the novelty of seeing two directors of experience having coffee earlier, with students on either side of them. He is struck by the fact that the general level of conversation of students with adults is much calmer. He's not 'hearing the shouting colleagues', he says. (He means, shouting at children.)

One unmissable change in the new building is that there is no queue of miscreants outside the leadership office, nor any of the 'weeping mothers' of whom John used to see so many. It is not his intention, says John, that the leadership team should be at arm's length, for parents or students. But the first port of call is the community.

There are continuing issues with ICT and a few other teething troubles. There were limited canteen choices for Years 7 and 8, when the contractors ran out of food. Four students from Jaguar, one of the senior communities, were caught trying to climb a fence. One boy got sent home, when he argued that since no member of staff wears school trousers, why should he? A girl who over the summer took an overdose has been causing problems all day, out of lessons and acting strangely.

One child told John that 'there's nowhere for me to hide'. But, he says, most are responsive to the new environment. 'The children are hugely respectful of what they have.' The learning communities 'have thrilled parents', says Janine Foale. In the end, 214 Year 7s arrived – well up on intakes in the last two years.

With much work done, there are three core elements to develop now, says John Matthews. The first is creating an organisation predicated on the needs of the individual. 'Teachers have said that the long lessons will be difficult. That comes from the perspective that the school is for adults. It is only a unit of time. It can be as flexible as the adult wants it to be.

'We now need to become an organisation where colleagues don't ask permission. I simply don't want colleagues to say "John! Is it OK if we do this?" I want them to be empowered, but from the perspective of the needs of the individual child.'

Point two, he says, is to continue to alter and improve the quality of relationships in school – all relationships, based on trust and respect. The new flatter leadership structure needs to be accompanied by a less hierarchical feel to the institution. 'Every role is an important one,' says John. 'There's no "I'm only..."'

'Everyone is pretty much on view, all the time,' he says. 'We model what we wish to see, in others.'

Point three is to push forward with changing what happens in classrooms. They, the leadership team, will be shadowing children, and spending time in classrooms. The interaction between teachers and students is the hardest aspect of school culture to change consistently, and arguably the most important. Teachers are under conflicting pressures – to push more students through conventional exams, at better grades. And to open out their practice to help young people take charge of their own learning in a deeper and more sustainable way.

The dynamic within the staff body generally has changed, the head believes. When the journey began, a proportion of staff were resistant to change. Some sat on the fence, unconvinced. Some were keen. In 2006, Ofsted judged that enough people believed in the ideas to make change possible. 'The leaders of Brislington Enterprise College are marked by a gritty determination,' inspectors wrote in their report. 'They believe passionately that all students can succeed.... A critical mass of staff are now following the strong and clear direction given by senior leaders.'

Two and a half years later, a higher proportion of staff are committed to the human scale principles and practice. Some of the critics have left. And a very few, admits John Matthews, 'are more entrenched in negativism'.

CHAPTER FIVE
Stantonbury Campus: a photo essay

by Mike Goldwater

Stantonbury Campus – a large comprehensive school in Milton Keynes – has been a bastion of progressiveness within English secondary schooling since it began, in 1974. Practice at the school has evolved over the years and taken different forms with different school leaders, staff and students but the founding principles of the institution have remained the same.

Core beliefs – established by the first principal Geoff Cooksey – are in 'equal value' and 'determined optimism' about the ability of all students to succeed. The notion of equal value underpins much of the practice at the school; staff and students are known by their first names, children do not wear school uniform and adults and children use the same lavatories and queue on equal terms for the canteen.

Stantonbury was divided into five Halls or mini-schools in the mid-90s, to foster closer relationships in the growing institution. The Halls, says current principal Mark Wasserberg, provide students with a secure, friendly base, an identity and sense of belonging – and the opportunity to compete with other Halls. The restructuring turned what is now a huge institution of 2,600 students into a more manageable and human scale one, using existing buildings.

'Determined optimism' in all children's ability to succeed is underpinned by teaching that attempts to meet the needs of individual students. Students in Years 7 to 9 undertake a variety of Rich Tasks that involve team-working and problem-solving on a real issue as the means of learning. Year 8 students in this photo essay on life at Stantonbury Campus are taking part in a Rich Task called 'Patterns, Sequences and Transformations – A Murder Mystery'.

'At the heart of Rich Tasks', says Mark Wasserberg, 'is the desire to make learning an active process for students that links to their lives and experience and which involves them in working together to solve problems and creatively demonstrate their learning.'

Practice at Stantonbury Campus continues to evolve. The challenge, says the principal, remains the one that arguably faces all schools. 'We need to do more to develop the understanding that first of all we teach children, not subjects.'

Year 8 class
(8SFA) with their
class teacher
Farina, Saxon Hall,
Stantonbury
Campus.

Kyla, Godwill and
Samantha arriving for
a science lesson.

At Stantonbury several subjects are linked
in a programme of problem-based learning
called 'Rich Tasks'. In the following
photographs, Year 8 work on a series of
clues to 'Patterns, Sequences and
Transformations – A Murder Mystery', using
skills learned in each of the subjects linked
to the task.

Prinal and Dexter
answer Rich Task
questions during an
art class.

In dance, Miranda
reads out her group's
Rich Task question
for Kyla to act out on
the floor.

Samantha, Laura
and Miranda work
out Rich Task
questions with
their maths
teacher.

Jade, Harleigh and
Helena discuss Rich
Task questions in
their science class.

Dominic talks
through a possible
solution to a Rich
Task question with
Callum while their
science teacher
listens to another
student.

Godwill, Prinal and
Dexter work on their
Rich Task in science
class.

Prinal completes
his Police Report
having solved the
Rich Task mystery.

James, Calum, Kiron, Dominic, Elliot, Sam and Callum hang out together during morning break.

Laura, who has help
with her reading,
works one-to-one
with her teaching
assistant.

Nicolle ices biscuits
in food technology
class.

Kieran and Elliot
eat in one of the
canteens with
their class teacher
Farina.

Helena reads
during afternoon
registration.

Suzanne and Amy
revise their science
work for an up-
coming test using
BBC Bitesize while
their science teacher
helps Jade and
Harleigh.

Students who need help
with their reading have
small group and one-to-
one sessions. Here the task
is to complete a paper
jigsaw puzzle that gives
instructions for making a
paper aeroplane, which
Laura is decorating.

Class teacher Farina
talks to Anisha and
her father during a
parents evening for
her class. Anisha's
younger sister
(wearing a pink
headscarf) will have a
session with her own
class teacher later.

Harleigh (centre)
organises a rehearsal
of a dance routine for
Red Nose Day with
Calum, Laura and
Helena.

Year 8 students
practise the
routine they have
devised for Red
Nose Day.

CHAPTER SIX
Brislington's journey

By January 2009, Brislington are into their third term (of a six term year), in the new building. The old school is all but demolished; it exists now only in the form of mountainous heaps of broken bricks and mortar, the physical matter of the old blocks broken up into ever smaller pieces by the contractors' heavy plant. With the site still carved in two, the approach to the new school remains awkward, a trek along a temporary walkway between high wooden hoardings. And the metaphor – of the transition process, of construction and decon-struction – persists, in the cultural transformation.

Inside the building, the personality of the college seems noticeably altered. Break times are calm. The street is flooded with whatever light is available outside and its cafes throng with students buying juices and paninis, alongside adults. There is still plenty of exuberant behaviour but it is different; adults and children are spatially more integrated here, more alongside each other. There is less sense that behaviour verges on being out of control.

The library – called the Enterprise Learning Zone – is centrally situated, in the middle of the street, next to the student entrance. Jess, a 16-year-old student from the Lynx special school community, is at the desk, taking out a book. She has cerebral palsy and was formerly in a segregated special school. In one corner, dressed in their own clothes, three sixth formers lend a collegiate air; a teacher is on his laptop in the middle of the space and elsewhere a Year 8 ICT class are working on one of four separate banks of computers, each large enough for a class group. Their teacher chivvies them along: 'Come on James! It is not acceptable after ten minutes not to know what you are doing.' This prominent, shared working space lends a feeling of maturity, sets a tone for the whole street.

Some of the issues arising from working in a leased building are making themselves felt. 'You come in early to do some work and the system might be down, or the laptops not working,' says one teacher. 'You have to log the problem, wait for an ID number, and then for the technician to come, later in the day. And things like the light from the window falling onto the whiteboard – before, you just spoke to the caretaker and he'd put up a blind.' Staff coffees are an issue, so is water. 'I don't find it very elegant to use the drinking fountain with the children. We need at least a water dispenser. I think water's not a lot to ask for.'

Since the new building opened four months ago, there has been a stream of visitors to the school. A party from Moscow, who want to partner with them as the Russian capital rebuilds its schools. People from the Qualifications and Curriculum Authority (QCA) arrived to talk about co-construction of the curriculum. A charity from Nepal came to see them, and students from the University of Reading. People from English schools want advice as they embark on the Building Schools for the Future process. Last November, Brislington won the BSF 'best school team' award, about which they were delighted. There's been a piece in the *South China Times...*

It is right that what is happening here should attract attention, for the scope of its ambition. Part of the rationale for inviting and hosting guests, says John Matthews, is to send a message to the students. 'It's about engendering pride.'

But while the build may be all but completed, the re-invention is – in some ways – just beginning. To do more than what one observer describes as 'herding children in a more benevolent way' takes time as well as the courage already evident.

standards agenda...

Brislington's drive to remodel itself as a human scale school has been undertaken first in the shadow – and now in the vice-like grip – of the standards agenda. The year group that departed the old school with such élan and joy last summer did not exit with the required achievements. By the old measures, Brislington has improved dramatically. The number of students leaving with five or more good GCSEs is up from 31 per cent in 2003 to 45 per cent in summer 2008. But only 27 per cent had five decent passes including maths and English (up from 15 per cent in 2003); the school's value-added score was the lowest for Bristol.

With the pressure already on, this was a further blow. That year group, says John Matthews, should have been at 53 per cent getting the five good GCSEs. As a school, they need to move fast to 65–70 per cent five A*–Cs, with 40–45% of those including maths and English GCSEs in the tally. While other things may be changing for the better for the children in the college, the Government requires marks-based evidence, in a hurry.

Education secretary Ed Balls told John Matthews personally when they met at a conference that the Government has 'drawn a line', under historic underachievement, under assumptions about 'kids like these'. John Matthews and his colleagues uphold – applaud even –

that line. But despite ditching such assumptions, the results at Brislington are not where they should be. Most painful to the leadership team was the fact that last year's 'value-added' score – the measure adjusted for the realities of a school's context – was low too.

A representative from the Department for Children, Schools and Families (DCSF) has been to see what they're doing. If they hadn't been able to articulate their educational vision convincingly to him, they might have been forced to become a National Challenge Trust school, says the head.

Separately, their new National Challenge adviser spent two days in school before Christmas. He told Janine Foale informally that he had thought before arriving it would be easy to identify what their issues were – but he couldn't immediately give them any more ideas than they already have.

John Matthews knows that historically teaching has not been consistently good across the school. One of his most shaming moments, he says, was when following the departure of Ofsted inspectors in 2002, a student told him enthusiastically: 'I've had a great week, sir. We've done some brilliant stuff, in lessons.'

Despite efforts since then to move to more student-centred, active styles of learning, there is still work to do. The leadership team have been holding two-day team reviews, bringing in external consultants to look at the performance of every department – and putting further pressure on teachers to animate and improve their practice. 'Colleagues know that if during review a lesson is deemed to be unsatisfactory, it initiates pre-capability procedures,' says the head. Such procedures can result in dismissal.

Teaching, their own figures tell them, is about 97 per cent satisfactory or better and 60 per cent good or better. The challenge they have set themselves is for teaching to be at a minimum of 80 per cent good, by October 2009. All their data, adds Janine Foale, suggests that where teaching is consistently good or excellent, the results are improving, at all levels of ability.

Three directors of experience have recently been energised by going on an 'Excellent teachers' course, in London, organised by London Challenge – a Government initiative to boost standards in the capital; the three are now holding workshops on the techniques with colleagues in after-school training sessions. One person is on stage one capability procedures – close to a real possibility of dismissal – after the review described a department that was 'inadequately led, incompetently managed'. A small number of people are on pre-capability procedures – a stage in which they are warned that their work must improve, and progress is monitored.

John Matthews and his senior colleagues believe they have done enough work, with teachers. Now, their message to them is: 'The journey has to be accelerated. Satisfactory teaching won't allow our children to make the level of progress they need.'

Not surprisingly, staff stress – as measured by sickness leave – has not so far decreased. The first months have been particularly demanding of staff, and continuing issues with ICT have not helped; the whole system went down when water leaked into the server at the hub of it. But the prime source of the stress is the requirement for consistently successful teaching that quickly manifests as improved test results.

Staff, says John Matthews, would say they as a senior management team are 'much harder'. 'I can't see where there are any excuses. Children are safe. Behaviour is much improved. Parents are choosing the school.' John Matthews reasons: if everything is in place – with relationships with children, sense of belonging, the place of the college in the community (not that this is resolved, nor do they pretend that it is) – then results should improve. 'It may well be', he says, 'that all the pieces are in place and it's now at a point where it's going to take off.'

year 8 English class...

In Cougar, after lunch, the acoustics on the upper floor are painful as raucous cries bounce off the stairs and landing walls. Students don't have to make much noise for it to sound like a din, remarks English teacher Jo Cross, ushering her Year 8 group into a classroom, urging them to keep trying to get their reluctant laptops logged on.

This top set for English is mainly composed of girls, working in groups around tables; one group have chosen to sit on the floor in a corner. Jo Cross moves around while they tell her what they're doing in their projects on analysis of media treatment of different groups. One group have chosen 'troubled celebrities'; they are searching online for stories about Britney Spears and Amy Winehouse. Another group are investigating media treatment of 'emos'. 'It stands for emotional. They're like – overwrought.'

A sticker on the front of Kayleigh's book says that she is at level 5B for English and that her target level is 6C. Will she get there? She shrugs. 'I like the longer lessons, because you only have to do three in a day. Before, we'd just get started and then we'd have to go.'

Jo Cross is in her fourth year at the school, and a member of Cougar. 'I'm much happier in the small community and mixing with the other members of staff. Especially this community seems to be very happy, most of the time. The difficult thing is being away from faculty members. We use email a lot more, or you have to wander down and find them. But before, we were quite isolated as a faculty. Now, there's more or less one person from every area of experience around you.'

Jo Cross spends 60 per cent of her time teaching in Cougar and 40 per cent outside, with GCSE and A-level students. 'I wouldn't want to give up teaching Key Stage 4, because of the enjoyment I get out of it, as well as career development,' she says. 'That's why I chose to be a secondary school teacher.'

With disappointing English results at the forefront of the National Challenge, Ms Cross and her colleagues are under particular pressure. The National Challenge adviser is a regular visitor, due again at the end of the week. The LA adviser was in last week, 'basically doing a mini Ofsted'. The School Improvement Officer came, plus there are peer observations, and leadership team observations. Ofsted themselves are expected any time. 'It's constantly forcing us to look at ourselves. I'm learning a lot more in this situation than I would otherwise. It is quite stressful. But there's no room for coasting along in a school like this.'

She believes the move to skills-based learning is yielding results. 'We're always trying to think of new ways of engaging the kids. That's what most teachers are concerned with at the moment. Enquiry-based learning does work, definitely. It's challenging, especially in Year 7, because our students are so low in confidence. But they really enjoy it and they're learning a lot. It lets them lead the lesson more.

'It's hard with the Year 11s. They have had five years of the scaffold being there for them and they're still quite low in confidence, some of them. Year 8s are a lot more independent – not afraid to give their ideas.'

Overall, she says the new organisation of the school is working to support her teaching. 'Being in Cougar is very positive, very supportive. You seem to spend a lot more time having individual conversations with children – because we're around them, we see them. And they know you better, so they're more inclined to come to you. The kids have character; there's a lot of banter, challenges every day – I just love that. And as a staff, you naturally become more supportive of each other.'

autonomy...

Ina Goldberg brings together Cougar's student council – a large group consisting mainly of girls, enthusiastic, well-equipped with pencil cases and coloured felt tips and marker pens – in the empty canteen area. Before they get to their list of ideas – about movies, dances, competitions – she encourages them to think about the purpose of the student council. The students say it is for 'helping people'. 'Respect within the community'. 'Student voice'. 'People call us nerds because we wear the badges,' one complains. And they get on with brainstorming about what they might make happen.

Cougar is developing a reputation within Brislington as a well-organised community. Ina Goldberg, head of Cougar, is working hard. She still teaches languages for one third of the timetable. In the first term, she wore a pedometer while at work; she walked 190 miles in this building – five or six miles a day.

She feels the new school has got off to a positive start. 'Kids like the set-up. They really do. I see a difference in the students. Especially with the ones more on the naughty side.' She cites a girl who has difficult issues to deal with in her home life, from a terminally ill parent to sexual abuse, and who in Year 7 was hardly ever present in lessons. This year, she is calmer, and appears happier. 'She feels so safe in this environment. She's in every day and goes to all her lessons. Last year, she didn't take part in school life at all. This year, she's been a delight.'

'That's the nice thing about the communities. The kids know that you know them. I know, when I walk up and down the street, who belongs to us, whether or not they're wearing their lanyards.'

Ina Goldberg would like the commitment to community-based learning at Brislington to go further. For the notion of collapsing the timetable to be practical, she says, Cougar teachers would need to be based full-time in the community – and to do that they would need to teach other disciplines. 'People should be teaching in their communities,' she says. 'It would mean people being more flexible, working outside their comfort zone. I think that's fine. We're teachers, we're here for the children.'

As things stand, teachers belong both to their communities, and to their subject discipline. But with their allegiances split, 'people don't belong 100 per cent to either their experience area or their community. They are torn in two different directions.' It opens up areas of confusion over responsibility, she says. And it dilutes community identity. As director of community, she has observed all the Cougar teachers teaching. For some, she would like to put in more coaching and development. But that treads on the toes of the directors of experience.

She is frustrated too that although the structures allow for regular observation of other teachers by all community teachers, only her community has made it compulsory for teachers to do so. But there is a price to pay for sticking to what you believe. 'If you do your own thing, what we're creating is like a comparison. People will compare, rather than belong. And the comparison creates frustration, upset and attitudes not positive to teaching.'

Four months in to the new school, relations between adults in the community are developing. 'They understand better where I'm coming from. And I understand more about where they're coming from.'

staff supporter...

In the street, Jane Graydon is dealing with a large boy who keeps throwing himself to the floor, to the amusement of his friends. 'You'll hurt yourself. What's the matter with you?' she says, grabbing his arm and sitting him down. Light streams through the glass walls, through the red and orange panels, casting pastel oblongs on the high white walls opposite, bathing passing students in radiance.

Jane Graydon still carries her brick-like walkie-talkie, but this building, she says, has made a difference to behaviour and in particular to truanting. 'They can't hide anywhere. I can see them, up and down. They can't go out.'

A group of Year 11 students comment that the main differences are that they can't smoke in the toilets any more, that there's no graffiti – because there are CCTV cameras and massive consequences – fewer fights, because they get broken up straight away. No head's detention, on a Friday. Instead, there is community service, cleaning the street, which is embarrassing. And no temptation – less, anyway – to truant, at least internally. 'Because there is nowhere to hide.' The phrase crops up all the time.

Students voice enthusiasm for their new surroundings, although the complaint is persistently made that it is 'like a prison'. The electronically locked doors can be opened by students' swipe cards – but only during their own break times. Some older students routinely kick open the fire doors at the back of the communities. They can smoke out of sight under the fire escapes – but still can't get off school premises from there.

I-base, the inclusion unit for children who either are asked to leave classes or have walked out, still has its clients; half a dozen children are working in here today, with a teacher who is based in the unit. 'This school is a prison,' says one. But whether because of the structure of the communities, the closed-circuit television, the locked doors – or the students' sense that they are respected, valued, by these new facilities, that lessons are more engaging and the communities safer places to be – behaviour has improved. One indicator is that Jane Graydon doesn't now receive the incessant staff support calls she used to get. 'It's better, my job's got easier,' she says. 'Staff are taking more responsibility. We're trying to get them not to use I-base as a dumping ground. It's for time out. If there's a major problem, I still go to them.'

Problems have not disappeared. Four children have been permanently excluded from the new school, one after he brought a knife into school. Another was excluded because he wouldn't wear the right trousers. 'We tried everything,' says John Matthews. 'But the mother's position was that until the staff wore uniform trousers, her son wasn't going to.' Would the boy have been permanently excluded from the old school? 'Probably not,' he says. Even the knife-carrier just might have been given another chance; at Brislington they genuinely like to hold on to their students wherever possible. But the culture of the new school is still being established, and certain principles – adherence to uniform, safety – must be seen to be non-negotiable.

Puma, the house for Years 9–11 and with the highest number of students and the highest proportion of more disaffected students, has not had an easy start. It is on to its second director after the first stepped down. A group of Puma's Year 11s are on a restricted timetable, only allowed in school from two in the afternoon until five.

The cohort at Brislington is changing. Whereas 13.8 per cent of the current Year 11s have special educational needs, around 33 per cent of the new Year 7s do. The proportion entitled to free school meals is 23.8 per cent across the school, but 27 per cent among the new intake of 11-year-olds. 'Our intake has shifted quite dramatically,' says John Matthews.

special needs…

A meeting in Lynette Newman's office makes plain that the issues the school has with troubled and unhappy young people are deep-seated and intractable. Simon Burrows, director of Jaguar community for Years 9 to 11, arrives. Jaguar's learning mentor is there and after a while the head appears too, apple in hand. They are talking about one of the boys who was in the restorative justice meeting with Jane Graydon last year. Mum had him arrested at the weekend, when she found cannabis in his room.

He's showing extreme anger, odd behaviour linked perhaps with use of skunk. He's overweight and doesn't have many friends, is too volatile to go on work experience. 'Have you got any answers?' asks Simon Burrows of the assembled adults. 'Because I haven't.'

'He sounds very like a CAF,' Lynette says. (A Common Assessment Framework procedure is meant to bring agencies such as health, education and social services together, to assess what help a young person needs.) The head proposes a risk assessment; the boy has been carrying weapons outside school. Simon Burrows is still contemplating what to do about his timetable. 'We need to have a conference with him that is completely non-threatening.'

They move on to talking about a girl who comes to school but attends few lessons and relates to almost no adults, especially male ones. Simon wants to arrive at a 'working scenario'. There is already a range of outside agencies involved with her. Counselling. School nurse. Social services. Family intervention and support. 'There are lots of things happening. But she is still coming to school and she's still an absolute nightmare,' says Simon Burrows. 'I don't know how to restrain her. She's walking away from all members of staff.' Social services are going to try and put her in foster care. 'But she'll probably walk.'

Simon is frustrated. There is no help in school, because her issues are not to do with her learning. She is bright. Able. Because she's on the child protection register, they can't send her home. 'Everything she sees just tells her that she's failing. Which is what she experiences at home.'

Lynette suggests that the girl start some vocational studies, early, combined with core subjects for GCSE. And can they customise her programme further, so that she is not expected to arrive until 10.25? If they don't, they will lose her anyway says John Matthews. 'She'll be out there and she'll be even more vulnerable.'

That's just two of them, Lynnette Newman comments at the end of the meeting. 'There are so many.'

Cougar community meeting...

Before Christmas, Cougar had a community meeting. The adults discussed what they thought was going well, in the formation of community identity and practice, and what they thought needed development. Now, in February, they are having a follow-up meeting. They begin the session by writing down what they believe 'community' means, prompted by a collage Cougar director Ina Goldberg gives as a hand out. Some members of Cougar arrive late, because they have been at faculty meetings. The community/faculty tension is ever present. One young teacher, asked which he felt he belonged to, shrugs and says 'in the end, neither'.

Groups then discuss different aspects of the human scale philosophy. 'Children learn best in small communities', is one of them. One teacher, a union representative, thinks the theory is sound. 'But much as it might suit children, it professionally limits staff so what we've ended up with is an imperfect model. It has to suit everyone.' She complains that although you may know the children in your community better, there become more children that you do not know at all – and therefore can't tackle if you see them causing problems.

Another statement up for discussion is that the model 'works best for poorer communities'. 'There's no doubt that parents are absolutely bowled over,' says one teacher, 'particularly in Year 7.' The Cougar adults move on to a table by table discussion of Cougar's emerging identity and practice. Under discussion are: duty black spots; training for the learning guide role; laptops not working; abuse of the ICT booking system; inconsistency over detentions; poor attendance at the girls' clubs; planners not being used as effective communication tools. 'Everything here is time,' says a young teacher. 'Sometimes working on community stuff feels as if it is detracting from subject input.'

A discussion on the wall displays in Cougar, and how to make time for the clerical person to improve them, leads into a discussion of how other communities are dealing with the same issue. And that leads into a broader discussion of communities not knowing each other's procedures. 'Do we have to know four different types of procedures, for different kids?' asks one. 'Yes we do,' comes the answer from another table.

Sarah Blainey suggests a 'welcome to Cougar' booklet, that sets out their procedures.

This painstaking building of trust and communication, alongside the practical workings of the community, is not easy in Bristol. American small school principal and writer Deborah Meier makes clear that it is not easy in Boston either. 'On my most discouraged days', she writes, 'I think what we're trying to do is probably impossible, but then I think that it's surely no more impossible than the dream of democracy writ large. It's a work in progress.'

parent voice

Donna Parkin's 11-year-old daughter began last September at Brislington. Why did she choose the school?

'I didn't, if I'm honest. If you live in this area, that's the school you're given. But parents in Year 8 said it was starting to turn around. And I knew about the new building – I was seduced by that, and by the talk the head gave when I came for an open evening.

'Before, too many children were left to run riot. I was delighted to see it had become schools within a school – that made the decision, from a parent point of view. Plus, don't get me wrong, she wanted to go there.

'My first concern was safety. And my second was behaviour. With it being in smaller communities, there's no hiding places. No doors on the toilet blocks. Everyone's in it together and they grow together. The community works very well. There's not that intimidation, where you're just swallowed up.

'She complains that dinner's too late – at 1.30, and there isn't a lot of food left. The thing she worries about in school is that there isn't enough fillings for the jacket potatoes. So that says it all really.

'I don't agree with enquiry-based learning. First, those with a tendency towards laziness won't do a thing. And my daughter's one of them. I prefer a lesson where the teacher is in control of his class and not the other way round. She'd be researching drama, dance, music … things she's interested in, not necessarily things she needs for future life skills.

'There's an assumption by the school that all children have a computer at home. But she doesn't. I think they need to address that. It's not all about ICT.

'I'm passionate about her education. I can see things that aren't functioning right, and I want to tell them. Like the induction pack not making sense. Answerphone messages not getting through. They've got to make sure that what they promise to parents as well as to children, they follow through. And they need to get the basics right. Give them what they need to get a job.

'She's happy, and that's what I want. A happy child. She saw one of her old classmates from primary school and the child said "your school's crap". My daughter said – "let's meet up in five years time and see who's got the best exam results."'

the teacher's story...

Ann Stobbs, 55, joined Brislington school as a young RE teacher and has recently been out for two years, on secondment to the 'extended schools project' – that works to bring services into schools to make them more accessible to children and families. She has come back to find children here changed. 'They are no longer prepared to listen,' she says. But there are compensations. Year 8s, she says, 'have loads of ideas'. They can 'talk for England'. 'They are skilled in working together.'

Ann Stobbs is a traditional teacher, working on changing her practice. 'The vision is for students to become independent learners, to take responsibility for learning, in partnership with teachers and parents. You work around where they're coming from, then try to take them into areas beyond their comfort zone. I've been aware of the developments, but the others are much more established in their practice than I am.'

Ann Stobbs believes in the changes, she says. 'A lot of the students lack confidence. Learning, further education, are not highly thought of in the area. It's a very safe, stable area, with traditional small businesses. A lot of parents have been through the school. The young people are beginning to get more confident. But there is a fair way to go and the exam system we have doesn't match in with them. It's too academic.

'The best thing we've done is the learning guide groups. They feel safer in them. As a tutor, I can contact parents more easily. It's not daunting. I've contacted more parents than previously, and I know students better. It doesn't feel as overwhelming – the level of need of response from just ten children. I can go and visit them in the classroom and I'm much more aware of their academic progress.'

Ann Stobbs trained before the introduction of the National Curriculum and says she enjoys the cross-curricular humanities. 'I've always liked the integrated approach. And it's good, talking about learning with others in the workbase. Teachers from different faculties are spread out across the communities and that's difficult. But there's a strong sense of community in Cougar. It's where I base myself, physically and emotionally. I find a lot of support there. We talk about our practices, about how people learn, what we could do. There isn't a culture of blaming students.

'Two years ago, the reputation of the school was poor. Two thirds of the kids locally went elsewhere. This year, there's been a huge increase in people wanting to come here. It's not just about the new building – it's about the small communities. The word on the street is that Brislington is changing. And it's true.

'What we haven't got right yet is the working with parents. It's still not enough. I still hear comments about "them" and expecting parents to come to "us". We are quite insular. Colleagues don't have the mindset for going out to the community.'

John Matthews...

Brislington Enterprise College is growing, in popularity and size. In 2006, just 142 students named Brislington as their first choice of secondary school. For autumn 2009, 217 have put the school first. There is an irony here; John Matthews and his colleagues began their quest to create a human scale school with the knowledge than the then large-sized school was perceived as too big, too impersonal. Numbers fell, as students and parents made other choices. Now, with the college organised as schools within a school, with small learning communities at the heart of its identity, numbers are again on the rise.

There is no resistance from the school; pupils bring money with them and rising numbers demonstrate much-valued community confidence. 'They should allow us to take all those who want to come here,' says the head. Still, this rebirth of the school is undertaken in perilous circumstances.

Brislington is ringed by new academies and faith schools. It is a hugely competitive situation and one of the possible scenarios is that Brislington – as the single remaining local authority comprehensive in the area – is required to take the students excluded or unwanted by the other schools. 'To my core, I want us to be inclusive,' says the head. 'But I'm not going to be used as a dumping ground.'

The senior leadership team are exploring – in advance of agreement from the governors – Trust status. 'Trust status could be win win,' says John Matthews; the City of Bristol would be part of the Trust but they should be able to have elements of control over their own direction, and buy in the best bits of the offer from Bristol.

'It would offer a level of resource we don't have. The governors would still be the governors. But equally – it could bring additionality. Within the community, there are resources.'

vision...

Is it possible, when constrained by the standards agenda, to create a truly human scale school? John Matthews keeps his eye on the longer term goal, as well as the immediate challenges. He quotes American school leadership guru Michael Fullan's notion of moral purpose. Collective moral purpose makes explicit the goal of raising the bar and closing the gap for all individuals and schools, says Fullan.

'We've decided to use the human scale education model in order to raise the bar, close the gap,' says John Matthews. 'We took a collective decision, that it was going to be different.

'Everything we're doing is about student wellbeing. In their future lives, by necessity, they have to have improved academic standards. Ofsted used to divide schools into those that were caring and those that were high achieving. We have to be both elements of that. We want to provide the highest level of care, for each individual. But equally that has to be about enabling students to achieve at the highest possible academic standards.'

They've worked physically very hard, he says, up to the move and over the time of the move. Much has been achieved and much remains to be done. Top of the agenda is a twin drive to improve teaching and to grow the partnership with parents and the community. There is much development potential as well on student voice, on enrichment activities, the emerging identities of the communities...

A senior student comes in asking for something and remains for some time, flicking her red hair extensions to and fro over her shoulders. John Matthews and Ruth Taylor chat animatedly to her. They relish her visit, her invitation to them to attend the Mexican evening her year group is putting on. A year ago, the head says when she leaves, this girl was 'massively angry'. Not now.

The reform of Brislington Enterprise College is a process, a work in progress. How is morale? 'We ebb and flow a bit,' says the head. 'The window of opportunity is narrowing, all the time. We need the oxygen of raised standards to buy time to implement the vision.'

Outside the window of this first floor office, at eye level, is what looks like a man-made mountain, a slag heap of unidentifiable origins. It's the old school. Not just pulled down now, but broken up. Graded and regraded says John Matthews, like a well-known brand of flour once used to be. He stands for a minute looking out of the window, at what will soon be sports pitches, arenas for triumph and defeat, for learning, for growth.

EPILOGUE

Mick Waters – formerly of Birmingham and Manchester education authorities and the QCA – addressing a Human Scale Schools conference at the end of 2008, described the historic role of schools as 'suppressors of young people'. A more relevant aspiration for schools now, he says, is that for young people they 'let me be me'. But even schools in the Human Scale Schools project are still by most measures some distance from that enlightened goal.

Mark Wasserberg, head of Stantonbury Campus, puts forward the difficulty of trying to create a caring but challenging educational culture, in an increasingly brutal context. 'Schools are still fundamentally instruments of social control,' he says. 'The real challenge is to move away from that. It strikes me increasingly as I get older that in England we don't like children very much. They are a problem to be solved.'

In a social context of increasing numbers of hurt and angry young people, human scale education may seem to be the most intelligent way of addressing schooling for all. But the political dimension – at its crudest, the need for vote-winning hikes in exam pass rates, achieved at whatever human cost – works directly against the innovative, courageous and time-taking remaking that education needs if it is to suit more children better.

When the HSS conference works in small groups on what the movement is about, they come up with one word. 'Relationships'. It is, they all feel, inadequate. But it is also important. Linda Nathan, inspirational co-head of the Boston Arts Academy (BAA) in the United States, who addressed the conference, defines her school's 3 Rs as 'relationship, relationship, relationship'.

The journey towards human scale education continues at Brislington Enterprise College, at Lister Community College and in different forms in other schools that are members of the Human Scale Schools project (see appendix). In some, the questions posed by Professor Michael Fielding of the Institute of Education, University of London, regarding Bishops Park College, are pressing: if a school's academic success is low, does it mean it is a failing school? How can a school's effectiveness be judged through non-quantitative means?

The work is everywhere more about reform than revolution. Head teacher Mark Wasserberg of Stantonbury Campus admits he and his colleagues are 'constantly compromising' with their students. The more radical aspirations of human scale education – co-construction of the curriculum, teachers working as confident partners in cross-disciplinary teams, development of alternative forms of assessment – are not much in evidence in the UK, although they are in the United States and elsewhere. Despite this, serious and courageous work is taking place and will bear fruit.

One crucial difference between the Boston Arts Academy and any English school is that BAA – with its 20 fellow 'pilot' schools – has a very high degree of autonomy, including in curriculum and assessment. In the absence – as yet – of a human scale academy in the UK, those involved in the Human Scale Schools project in England might borrow the habits of mind adopted by staff and students at Linda Nathan's Boston school.

'RICO' stands for Refine, Invent, Connect, Own…

Refine: Have I conveyed my message? What are my strengths and weaknesses?

Invent: What makes this work inventive? Do I take risks and push myself?

Connect: Who is the audience and how does the work connect? What is the context?

Own: Am I proud of the work I am doing? What do I need to be successful?

READING LIST

Davies, M., *Human Scale Education: Human Scale by Design* (Human Scale Schools Project, 2009).

Fielding, M., Elliot, J., Burton, C., Robinson, C. and Samuels, J., *Less is More? The Development of a Schools-within-Schools Approach to Education on a Human Scale at Bishops Park College, Clacton, Essex* (London, Institute of Education, 2006).

Meier, D., *In Schools We Trust: Creating Communities of Learning in an Era of Testing and Standardization* (Boston, Beacon Press, 2002).

Sizer, T., *Horace's Compromise: The Dilemma of the American High School* (New York, Houghton Mifflin, 1984).

Sizer, T., *Horace's Hope: What Works for the American High School* (New York, Houghton Mifflin, 1996).

Tasker, M., *Human Scale Education: History, Values and Practice* (Human Scale Schools Project, 2008).

Online publications:

Children's Society, *A Good Childhood: Searching for Values in a Competitive Age* (2009):
www.childrenssociety.org.uk/all_about_us/how_we_do_it/the_good_childhood_inquiry/1818.html

Department for Education and Skills, *2020 Vision: Report of the Teaching and Learning in 2020 Review Group* (2006):
http://publications.teachernet.gov.uk

Joseph Rowntree Foundation, *Tackling Low Educational Achievement* (2007):
www.jrf.org.uk/publications/tackling-low-educational-achievement

Royal Society of Arts, *Opening Minds Framework*:
www.thersa.org/projects/education/opening-minds-old/opening-minds-framework

Teach First, *Lessons from the Front: 1,000 New Teachers Speak Up*
(2007):
www.teachfirst.org.uk/news/policyfirst

UNICEF, *Child Poverty in Perspective: An Overview of Child
Well-being in Rich Countries* (2007):
www.unicef-irc.org/publications/pdf/rc7_eng.pdf

Websites:

Calouste Gulbenkian Foundation:
www.gulbenkian.org.uk

Human Scale Education:
www.hse.org.uk

Small Schools Workshop, United States:
www.smallschoolsworkshop.org

APPENDIX

Schools funded by the Human Scale Schools project

Lead Schools for the HSS Network:
Brislington Enterprise College, Bristol
Stanley Park High School, Carshalton, Surrey
Stantonbury Campus, Milton Keynes
Walker Technology College, Newcastle upon Tyne

School funded in April 2009
St Aelred's Catholic Technology College, Newton-le-Willows, Merseyside

Schools funded in November 2008
Cardinal Newman Catholic School, Luton, Bedfordshire
Washington School, Tyne and Wear

Schools funded in November 2007
Farnley Park High School, Leeds
Stanley Park High School, Carshalton, Surrey

Schools funded in July 2007
Hove Park Language College and Sixth Form Centre, East Sussex
The Netherall School, Cambridge
Varndean School, Brighton, East Sussex
Walker Technology College, Newcastle upon Tyne

Schools funded in March 2007
Astley Sports College, Dukinfield, Cheshire
Chorlton High School, Manchester
Christ's College, Guildford, Surrey
Coombeshead College, Newton Abbot, Devon
Cramlington Community High School, Northumberland
Haybridge High School and Sixth Form, Hagley, Worcestershire
Holyhead School, Handsworth, Birmingham
Lister Community School, Plaistow, London
Northampton School for Girls, Northampton
St John's School and Community College, Marlborough, Wiltshire
Somervale School, Midsomer Norton, Bath

Springwell Community School, Chesterfield, Derbyshire
Tideway School, Newhaven, East Sussex
Trinity School, Carlisle, Cumbria
Woodlands School, Basildon, Essex

Schools funded in November 2006
Burlington Danes Academy, London
Freebrough Specialist Engineering College, Brotton, Cleveland
The Thomas Lord Audley School and Language College,
    Colchester, Essex

Schools funded in July 2006
Abbeydale Grange School, Sheffield
Didcot Girls' School, Oxford
Hartsdown Technology College, Margate, Kent
The Westlands School, Sittingbourne, Kent
Wilsthorpe Business and Enterprise College, Longeaton, Nottingham

Schools funded in March 2006
Allerton Grange School, Leeds
Brislington Enterprise College, Bristol
Glossopdale Community College, Glossop, Derbyshire
Hugh Christie College, Tonbridge, Kent
Montgomery High School, Blackpool, Lancashire
Artists in Schools: Bolton, Bury and Rochdale, Lancashire

The Human Scale Schools project is co-ordinated by Human Scale Education for the Calouste Gulbenkian Foundation. The project is also supported by the Esmée Fairbairn Foundation and the Paul Hamlyn Foundation.

Human Scale Education, Unit 8 Fairseat Farm, Chew Stoke, Bristol
BS40 8XF
01275 332516
info@hse.org.uk
www.hse.org.uk

Wendy Wallace has long experience in writing about education and has contributed to numerous national newspapers, and magazines. As a feature writer for The TES she wrote extensively on leadership, social affairs in education, and education policy and practice. In 2001, she was Education Journalist of the Year. Her book on life in an inner city primary school, *Oranges and Lemons*, was published by Routledge in 2005 and her book on abandoned children in Sudan – *Daughter of Dust* – by Simon & Schuster in 2009.

Mike Goldwater is an international photojournalist whose pictures have been published in major magazines around the world. A co-founder of photo agency Network Photographers – which built an international reputation for photojournalism of the highest quality – his book on water, *Acqua*, was published in Milan in 2002. He fulfils corporate and editorial assignments for a range of clients and his work can be seen at www.mikegoldwater.com.